CLOUDS
IN THE
WEST

Lessons from the Martial Arts of Japan

DAVE LOWRY

THE LYONS PRESS
Guilford, Connecticut
An imprint of The Globe Pequot Press

For the Reverend Canon D.H. Skoyles, who, as this book was completed, celebrated his final Solemn High Mass in a manner no doubt indistinguishable from that in which he shall continue to wield his sword: *suaviter in modo, fortiter in re.*

The Lyons Press is an imprint of The Globe Pequot Press.

10 9 8 7 6 5 4 3 2 1

Printed in the United States of America

ISBN 1-59228-590-2

Library of Congress Cataloging-in-Publication Data is available on file.

To buy books in quantity for corporate use or incentives, call **(800) 962–0973, ext. 4551,** or e-mail **premiums@GlobePequot.com.**

From the depths of my heart
The beautiful snow
Clouds in the West

Kokoro kara
Yuki utsukushi ya
Nishi no kumo

                    —Issho

Contents

Introduction   vii

1. *Kufu* (Solving a Quandary)   1

2. Ittosai's Test   13

3. *Igen* (Dignity)   27

4. *Nakaima* (The Eternal Present)   39

5. A Matter of Bathrobes . . .   53

6. *Iai* (Unsheathing the Sword)   63

7. *Gaman* (Perseverance)   75

8. Sensei   87

9. What's in a Name?   103

10. *Nangyodo* (The Way of Hardship)   113

11. Mythic Origins of the Ninja   125

12. To Blossom and to Scatter . . .   139

13. Polishing the Mirror, Creating the Kata   155

Dave Lowry

14. Classical Japanese Martial Arts in the West:
    Problems in Transmission   165
15. Confessions of a Navy SEAL   187
16. Kata as a Protection against the Arbitrary 201

Introduction

The demonstration of *budo* we were presenting last year was for a local *Nihonjin-kai,* a social club for Japanese expatriates. Not surprisingly, given the fact that I and a couple of my training partners were all non-Japanese presenting a traditional Japanese art to a largely Japanese audience, there were several questions after the demonstration. One man prefaced his question by noting that he was a keen chess enthusiast and went on to make an extended and inaccurate analogy between the strategy of chess and the movements of the *kata* he had just seen us do. I responded, when he finally took a break in his meandering monologue, with the suggestion that he learn to play *go.*

Another man asked how it was that I had become involved in disciplines the practical utility of which were only slightly less relevant than their status in the country that spawned them, arts that ceased any realistic aim of being brought to their intended conclusion more than a century ago. Good question. I have been asked it before. My only response is that if anyone can reach the age of forty or so and can explain exactly why and succinctly how they managed to get to where they are, then they have probably lived fairly boring lives. And then a woman asked how long I had been doing budo. I began training in 1968, I said. In a voice loud enough to be heard throughout the room, she exclaimed, "That was before I was born!"

From the perspective of that young woman—and I emphasize, she was really, really young—I have been following the path of the Japanese budo for a long time. From my own perspective, honestly and without the pretense of false modesty, I would acknowledge that I am beyond the beginner stage. But not much beyond. I have passed through the gate—and that is about all.

I do not remember when this happened. When I first entered a dojo, I knew beyond any doubt it was a place where I belonged, and I never looked back. So I could not say in retrospect when I passed beyond being a beginner, a *monjin,* a "person at the gate," and went on in. But somewhere along the path, I do know that budo became less "special." This may sound odd. That which we love and follow would seem to become just the opposite: more special the more we are exposed to it, the more it becomes part of our lives. When I say the budo became less special, however, what I mean is that at some point, it was no longer an "exotic" thing. At the start, the odd uniform, the strange training weapons, the unfamiliar language and customs all seemed extraordinary. Over time, the rituals of practice, the sight of a wet *keikogi* hanging out under the eaves to dry, the terminology—all became a part of my daily life. I made my bed in the morning; I went to practice in the evening. As the years passed, these became more or less the same in my daily activities.

The word in Japanese is *tsune.* "The usual state of things" is one translation. Tsune is "the ordinary." The budo, over time, became tsune in my life. I cannot imagine what my life would be without them, any more than I can imagine what it would be like to not check the mailbox for mail in the afternoon or to not eat breakfast. In my opinion, if the budo are to have any real value for us, they must be tsune in our lives. Not some special event that has us barefoot and dressing funny and performing arcane exercises at the "class" we attend a couple of nights a week, but a fundamental aspect of our existence.

The inspiration for the title of this collection was taken from a poem written by Kosugi Issho at the time of his death in the winter of 1688. Issho was a tea merchant in Katamachi, a town located in present-day Kanazawa Prefecture. Seriously ill, he was determined to write a long series of linked verses in honor of his deceased father, even though his friends warned him the strain of composition would be too much him. Probably suffering from tuberculosis, he passed out several times during the task and was often found gasping for breath. Issho finished, however, and those with him at the time noted that his countenance suddenly became serene, seeming to radiate energy. He composed his death poem, then passed on, composed and dignified.

I have an utter faith in an eternal and blissful afterlife. Even so, when my time comes, I'm likely to be ranting and grabbing for any chance at one more breath, complaining bitterly and whining and feeling sorry for myself. Whatever I manage to muster of any sort of composure or dignity like Issho, much of my ability to do so will have come because of the kind of structure the budo have given me. That structure is what gives these unique arts their deepest meaning and value. When we make them tsune, an integral part of our lives, we begin to build that inner structure.

The phrase "clouds in the West" can be interpreted several ways in Issho's poem and as it occurs in other Japanese literature. He may have meant it as a reference to the angelic emissaries that are supposed to come from that direction to meet the newly dead when they depart this earth for the Buddhist Paradise in the West. For me, *nishi no kumo* is an evocative image.

When I was very young, I stood on the top of one of the low, rolling hills of southern Kansas and watched enormous cumulonimbus clouds pile up on the western horizon, thick and billowing, so dazzlingly white at their crowns they hurt the eyes to look at them, bruised dark as ripe blackberries on their low bellies. Sometimes the clouds brought needed rain. Other times, it was lightning or hail pinging off roofs and smashing crops.

Japan is so far to our West that it is East. Still, it is from that direction that things Japanese have tended to come to us. The budo have come like those clouds in the West I saw as a child. They have a similar potential. They can have a tremendously positive influence, or they can be destructive. Or, like some of those massive clouds, they can just evaporate and disappear or pass over and be gone. In the essays that follow, I have observed each of these forecasts as they have unfolded. I hope you will read and enjoy them and decide how accurate a prognosticator I am. I am less a meteorologist than I am a martial artist. Yet I continue to watch those clouds gather and roll in, excited by their promise, awed by their power, content to know that they are a part of my daily life.

Written at *Geshi*, Summer Solstice, 2004

1

Kufu

Solving a Quandary

Do not thrust the spear with the hands. Neither with the mind. Thrust without thrusting. Think without thinking.

> —an oral teaching of the Hozoin ryu

It is not logical. But it is so.

> —Mister Spock

He was one of the most talented and gifted of the younger generation of *karateka* I'd ever seen. Charging across the dojo floor, his lanky frame—once the epitome of awkward, adolescent geekiness—had been educated and trained. In three years, I had seen Tom progress from a skinny nerd into a confident, self-possessed young man. It showed in his demeanor. It showed, too, in his karate. His reaction times were refined, and he became more supple; his muscles carried him through a training session with a powerful efficiency. Once he was promoted to *shodan,* the first level of black belt, his enthusiasm increased.

This is not always the case. In many instances, karate practitioners who are awarded a black belt feel they have reached a goal and may slack off or even quit training altogether, never realizing they have only reached the point where their serious training can commence. Not Tom. He rarely missed a class. He punched and kicked with concentrated force and admirable energy. He gave even some of the seniors in the dojo some tough competition in sparring. Outside the dojo, Tom was learning to apply the tough lessons of budo to his daily life. He'd just graduated high school near the top of his class. He had more than half a dozen scholarships to choose from for college.

But Tom couldn't do the kata *Tekki nidan*.

Tekki nidan, or *naifanchi nidan*, is the second of three related forms. All are short in length. None are terribly complicated. Tekki nidan is often taught at about the time a karateka is promoted into the black-belt ranks. Unlike most of the other kata of karate, the series of Tekki don't require the performer to move in multiple directions executing the techniques of the kata. Instead, they call for only a single stance, the *kiba dachi*, or straddle-leg stance, and the performer moves laterally on one line, back and forth. Tekki nidan demands some strong legs, precise actions, and an unbroken concentration to master its various techniques. But Tom was already well on his way to polishing those aspects of the kata. His problem was far less complex—or, it would seem, at least less challenging. He could not, after repeated, intensive practice stretching over several months, return to the same place when he finished the kata at which he had started.

The *embusen*, or "performance line" of kata, is designed to bring the practitioner, when he concludes the movements of the kata correctly, back exactly to the point where he started. When or why this convention in karate kata began is, so far as I know, a mystery. Those who insist it is a modern innovation—meant to make it easier for large classes to train simultaneously in restricted spaces—must explain why the start/stop place is similarly fixed in Chinese arts like *taiji* and other such formal exercises that have been practiced for centuries. No matter. The fact is, the kata has to start and stop at the same place to be "correct." If you end up in a different place from where you started, not only is your kata aesthetically lacking in some way, it's also a good clue that you are doing something wrong. Some of your steps may be too short or long, or you may be leaving out a sequence. Something needs work. Being able to execute a kata so it begins and ends at the same spot is not proof you've mastered the kata—but *not* being able to stop where you started is a definite indication you have not.

In Tom's case, beginning and concluding Tekki nidan correctly should not have been an insurmountable obstacle. The kata doesn't exactly call for the karateka to be moving all over the place. There are no spectacular jumps as in *Kanku*. No intricate body shifts like in *Bassai*. Just four steps to the right, if you break the kata down and examine it, and four back to the left. There are a couple of steps requiring one to shift, crossing one leg over the other, and that's it. Simple. Not for Tom, however. No matter how many times he went through it, he was always one step too far to the right when he finished the kata.

At first, Tom assumed he was leaving out a movement or perhaps putting in an extra one along the way. He stopped to watch his classmates in the dojo. He double-checked a book on the kata. He found that in fact, he was performing all the techniques called for and doing them in the proper order. He tried again, and again he was off—and always by the same step. After the class ended, Tom rushed to the dressing room with an idea. He took his shoes and moved them on the floor, precisely in the same spacing as if he were in them and doing the kata. As he'd theorized, the shoes ended up off the starting-point line by the same distance his feet were off when he'd performed Tekki nidan in the dojo. Triumphantly, he approached the sensei. He had proof. Unless the Tekki performer somehow altered his stances, closed up or stretched out his steps in some way, it was impossible for the form to end where it started. The sensei nodded understandingly. He called out to one of the seniors, still practicing out on the floor. "Tekki nidan, please," he asked. The senior took a spot on the floor and went through the kata slowly. "Tell me, Tom," the sensei said, "when you see him changing the distance of his stances." The senior finished the kata, never varying his stances by so much as an inch as far as Tom—or any of the rest of us watching—could tell, and he finished Tekki exactly where he began it.

As part of a high school project, Tom had designed his own computer program. It was enormously complex—he tried to describe it to me a couple of times and was completely over my head—involving calculations and mathematical formulas that would utterly bewilder most of us. But he still couldn't figure out how the heck Tekki nidan was to be done, and his frustration was both evident and growing.

"Sensei!" the usually quiet young man exploded. "Please tell me what I'm doing wrong! I've thought of everything and none of it is working."

"You're not doing it right then," replied the sensei.

"But I can't think of any other possible way," came Tom's earnest response.

"Then quit *thinking* and *do it!*"

Generally speaking, the most basic thought process of Western civilization is something we might call "equation reasoning." An example of equation reasoning is "All boys are men. Bob is a boy. Therefore, Bob is a man." Since long before the days of Aristotle, we've grown up learning various forms of this equation. Toddlers learn "I want candy. The way to get candy is by asking *please*. Therefore, may I please have some candy?" At this level, reasoning through constructing an equation seems pretty simple. It may be. But in fact, it pervades our society in all kinds of ways, and I am glad of it.

The logic of such equations must be considered at least one of the reasons why Western civilization has been responsible for the majority of material improvements in the history of the world. From the formation of representative governments, to economic theory, to industrialization, the equation method of reasoning has brought about advancements that have made the world a far better place than our ancestors ever could have hoped for. Heated water produced steam, someone discovered. And, although it took a while, someone else eventually reasoned that steam could be channeled to make pistons or turbines move. And in a relatively brief span of time we progressed from simple tabletop toy machines fueled by steam to engines similarly powered and capable of running ships and locomotives.

The same kind of reasoning led to the conclusion that all humans were indeed created equal in the eyes of their fellow man, and since blacks and other minorities were human, they ought to be afforded the same rights and responsibilities as everyone else. To be sure, this was a halting, sometimes endangered summation. There were steps backward as well as forward. Nonetheless, at least in part through the method of equation reasoning, a tremendous advancement in human rights was made.

Of course, like any system of thought, equation reasoning has its limitations. If A equals the sum of B and C, then accordingly, it ought always to be so and always dependable as such. Further, we who depend so heavily on it tend to be thrown into confusion and are sometimes stymied when the system fails us. One can imagine the final, bubbling thoughts of one of our early ancestors who attempted to cross a river by leaping astride a tree trunk floating by, unaware that it was completely saturated and waterlogged—"But all the other ones floated before!"

Before he could speak he'd discovered that crying brought food, solving the problem of hunger for the foreseeable future, and so for Tom, the natural recourse to his problem with the kata was to turn to the system of logic that worked so well up to this point. Yet as Tom is going to discover in other aspects of his life as it goes on, the tools of linear logic and equation reasoning are not always up to the jobs we encounter. In the case of Tekki nidan, Tom could have examined the kata logically from every possible angle, never getting it to make sense, as he understood "sense" to be. And yet he was faced with the irrefutable truth that the kata did work. His seniors were still out on the dojo floor, going through the movements of Tekki nidan, and they were all finishing in the correctly prescribed place.

The sensei, because he was a sensei, understood that useful though they are, logical equations have their limitations. Rather than employing merely the intellect, he wanted Tom to tackle the kata with his whole being. To accomplish this, Tom would have to set aside his brainpower for a while. He needed to suspend his intellectual processes. He needed to resort to *kufu*—finding his way out of a quandary by tapping into the intuitive part of himself.

The ability to approach a problem through kufu is not easy. There aren't many accomplishments in one's budo training that are more profound. It is a releasing of the most elemental of man's energies toward the goal of solving a problem that simply cannot be conquered by conventional, rational means. There are all kinds of legends about the swordsman Miyamoto Musashi and his victories over multiple opponents. In these stories, Musashi is always surrounded by enemies bent on his death. No matter how you look at it, Musashi's time appeared to be up in these situations. Somehow, though, Musashi turns to kufu, and prevails. In one famous narrative, it was just such a moment that inspired him to draw his second, shorter sword and use it in conjunction with the longer one to defeat his opponents. The story probably isn't true in some, even many, of the details. There isn't much evidence Musashi ever used two swords in such duels. But there is little doubt that Musashi was capable of bypassing linear logic at times to come up with an inspiration that saved his life— or at least solved an apparently insurmountable problem through the intuitive process of kufu.

A more verifiable instance of kufu is found in the early career of Jigoro Kano, the founder of judo. It was in his years as a student of the Kito ryu of jujutsu. Kano was—isn't this always the case with young martial artists?—a frail kid. At the time he was training in the Kito ryu dojo, he weighed less than one hundred pounds. Nothing wrong with that, particularly. But it presented a certain challenge to Kano since one of his daily training partners, Kenkichi Fukushima, was over six feet tall and burdened the scales with more than two hundred pounds. The strategy of the Kito ryu called for a smaller man to defeat a larger one through either deflections of an attack or entering in at a critical angle, to tackle or throw or strike. Kano was skilled in many of the Kito ryu techniques designed according to these strategies. Against Fukushima, though, none of them worked.

Kano took the usual route in dealing with this quandary. He studied old jujutsu scrolls, consulted a retired *sumotori* for tips, and delved into texts on Western wrestling. He experimented and researched. Kano would later become famous not only in Japan but also internationally for his skills as an educator. He is the first Japanese to have comprehensively studied Western teaching methods, and his commentaries are still read by those in education. (During my own undergrad days, majoring in English education in the 1970s, we had to read Kano's writings on pedagogy.) So it was natural for Kano to employ an intellectual and rational approach to his problem with Fukushima. In the end, though, this wasn't enough. Kano's solution came during a bout with Fukushima. Frustrated, he abandoned logic and the Kito ryu's strategy of attacking at an oblique angle. Instead, he drove straight in against Fukushima, attacking directly. He dropped to one knee, holding one of Fukushima's sleeves and grabbing his opponent's leg. Standing and hoisting Fukushima across his shoulders, Kano wheeled and threw the giant to the mat in a dramatic arc. Through kufu, Kano solved his problem. The result was his creation of a new throw, *kata guruma* (shoulder wheel), still commonly practiced in judo all over the world.

Kufu is written in Japanese with a couple of characters that, if we trace them far enough back, come from a pictograph of a man combined with a carpenter's square. In other words, "a guy with a tool for getting something done." In everyday parlance in Japanese, that's what kufu means, more or less. It is a plan or a strategy. The meaning it has for us as *budoka* comes to some extent from its employment in the discipline of Zen. (D. T. Suzuki, in his famous book, *Zen and Japanese Culture*, writes about kufu as if it were the sole province of Zen training and ascribes to it a lot of mystical connotations. This is not entirely correct. Zen teachers adopted the term from ordinary Japanese, and later on they and others, like Suzuki, attached to it the special meanings we're discussing here.) In Zen training, kufu is most closely associated with the *koan*.

Most readers are familiar with koan. Aside from their use in providing inane chitchat for Zen dilettantes and material for fatuous books written by the same, a koan is designed to bring the Zen disciple into a confrontation with kufu. "What was your face before you were born?" asks the *roshi*, or Zen priest, and his student is, understandably, at a loss for a coherent reply. If he tries to answer in a scientific mode, explaining that his face was composed of the chromosomes of his parents, the roshi is very likely to whack him with a stick. If he speaks in some kind of New Age psychopiffle, he's laughed at. Or hit again. No matter how he answers, his responses are wrong and ridiculed or ignored. He is instructed only to meditate on his koan, to make it the sole focus of his training and daily life.

In the old days, koan training was almost inhumanly severe. At times, disciples were brought nearly to the point of death in their efforts to solve the question. Its adherents don't like to talk about it and Westerners in love with Zen tend to be unaware of it, but even today in Zen temples, koan can result in illness and intense emotional or psychological problems. If the Zen trainee is able to overcome his dependence upon logic and reasoning, however, and absorb himself in the koan with his entire spirit, it often happens that an answer erupts from deep inside him. The answer will not be logical, mind you. It isn't like solving a riddle. The answer, in fact, may be in the form of a shout. Or in a solution that's apparently just as meaningless as the original question. It won't matter what words or sounds or actions constitute the answer. What matters is that the teacher recognizes that the student has reached beyond logic and found another depth of his consciousness. He has found kufu and in doing so, come closer to being able to use the medium of kufu at will, to experience, as a result, life at a more meaningful level.

For the martial artist, the kata are a sort of dynamic koan. Even if Tom solved the problem presented by the seemingly impossible footwork of Tekki nidan (he did), he would soon discover there are even more difficulties in kata training that seem to defy logical solutions. These koan are out there, lurking for every budoka. The karateka going on his merry way, for instance, assuming that he understands a particular sequence in a kata as a defense against an attack, will be interrupted by his teacher. The sensei will, without warning, ask the karateka to demonstrate the sequence, against an attacking partner. The movement he's carefully practiced will be set up, the attacker will cooperate. But the sequence will fail. It just doesn't work the way the karateka believed it would. This can be discouraging. Yet it is, in reality, merely another koan that has been put in his path. He may be able to solve this one intellectually, work it out logically. But he may also find that it is another opportunity to develop his kufu.

Seeking an answer through means other than rational reasoning is not wholly foreign in Western philosophy. Approaches similar to kufu occur in a number of realms of Western religions and philosophical systems. The Christian philosopher Soren Kierkegaard postulated that should an individual believe he was capable, on his own, of accomplishing a lifetime of good, eventually he would be forced to change his mind—dramatically so in some cases. Faced with all the evil around him and within himself, he would have no choice. Confronted with the overwhelming evidence of his own inability to solve the problem of evil, Kierkegaard suggested man would eventually have to take a "leap of faith," jumping into the arms of God, trusting entirely to a higher power in meeting life's travails. What Kierkegaard was describing, some might argue, is a sort of Christian approach to kufu.

Even though examples of kufu exist in Western thought, it is through a serious encounter with the budo that many non-Japanese are introduced to the concept. Given our heritage of logic and rational reasoning, there can be a lot of resistance to the notion. At every step, when we run into difficulties in the dojo, we are tempted to resort to our comfortable modes of working out problems intellectually. And of course, intellection has its place and is valuable for us. But when it fails to give us the answer we need, we must press on. We must practice our kata, immerse ourselves in the training as if these constitute our own, personal koan. We need to strive for solutions that cannot be discovered through our logic. This is a much more difficult process than it might appear, as people like Tom can tell you. Kufu is, I suspect, the goal sought by a swordsman of old Japan, who wrote this poem, describing his own inner struggle with the Way:

Under the sword lifted high,
There is hell making you tremble.
But push on,
And you will enter a land of bliss.

2

Ittosai's Test

As he approaches the end of his productive teaching career, every master of every art must come to grips with a difficult problem. He is faced with the task of selecting a worthy successor or successors to carry on his teachings. Often, this will be the culmination of his experience in the art. The true master, whether his Way is that of the tea ceremony, or flower arranging, or *Noh* drama, will know that evidence of his skills is at best, ephemeral. Even masters of calligraphy or pottery will leave behind only so much concrete evidence of their work, and those scrolls or bowls will eventually disintegrate or break. All that can truly exist with any hope of permanence is the legacy the master leaves behind in the generation of his students.

This is particularly true in the case of the martial Ways, and it must have been an even more critical concern during Japan's feudal age when the art of swordsmanship was literally a matter of life and death. Using a sword was a combative necessity for the professional warrior class, the samurai. In many instances the reputations of those ryu devoted to its practice rested almost entirely on the character of the school's headmaster. In those cases where the headmaster was infirm or crippled or otherwise clearly not a representative of the ryu in a technical sense, maintaining the status of the ryu would be the responsibility of the senior practitioners. So in either case, the concern for passing along the secrets and lore and techniques of a ryu in their entirety was not to be undertaken lightly. If a ryu had a large number of exceptional students, the master could take his time, carefully shepherding progress and evaluating the potential of a crop of aspirants. Of course, in many martial ryu, headmastery was automatically conferred upon the eldest son of the school's master. This conveniently narrowed the choice for the ryu's successor. And if, as it sometimes happened, the son was not terribly impressive or skilled in his father's art, the father would make certain to have a gathering of the school's best exponents around his offspring. They served in one way or another as unofficial leaders and instructors, thus maintaining the school's reputation.

But as the last drifts of the wet, gray snow of the winter melted away in the sixteenth year of Tensho (1588), the swordsman Ito Ittosai Kagehisa could depend neither on a large and healthy crop of prospective successors among his students nor on a family heir ready to take over his Itto ryu. He had only two disciples from whom he could choose to carry on the traditions and strategies of his system of combat with the sword. One was Migogami Ono Tenzen, a young samurai attached to the Satomi clan, known for his fiery temper. The other was Zenki, a ferryman who, while rowing him across a river, had challenged Ittosai. Kagehisa easily defeated Zenki once they reached the opposite shore, but, impressed with the ferryman's attitude, he accepted Zenki as his first student.

Kagehisa, the founder of the Itto ryu, was, to put it as gently as possible, an interesting character. To be more honest, he was an eccentric nutball. He was a brilliant swordsman, to be sure. His Itto ryu would eventually be adopted by the Tokugawa shogun as one of the two "official" schools of swordsmanship under the direct patronage of the shogunal government. Even with such successes, he was enigmatic. His behavior was often bizarre by the conservative standards of his era. So when it came time to choose a successor, no one who knew of Kagehisa's history would have been surprised that the master chose an extreme method to make the decision.

Martial historians of Japan suggest much of Kagehisa's character was formed by the early deaths of his parents. An orphan, he was raised by a priest at the Mishima temple, in a village on the coast of the Izu Peninsula, on the southern part of the main island of Japan. From fairly early on in his life, Ittosai—then known by the childhood name of Yagoro—apparently was preoccupied with the sword. He swung a wooden stick for hours each day, fighting mock duels with companions or battling against tree branches or boulders when he was alone. At around the age of fifteen, his swordplay took a more serious turn. Thieves appeared at the Mishima temple, intent on ransacking the place for whatever they could find. Expecting to find it defended only by some of the elderly monks, they were not prepared for the young Kagehisa, who waded into the group, wildly swinging his stick with such enthusiasm that they were driven off the temple grounds in a panic. In gratitude for defending the temple, the priest gave Kagehisa a sword and enough money to start him off on a search for a competent teacher to show him how to properly use the weapon.

Whether or not Kagehisa planned to do just that is anyone's guess. For an orphan kid, off on his own, experiencing life's temptations and opportunities outside the walls of a temple—maybe Kagehisa found other ways to spend the money or his time. Whatever he did, he eventually ended up in Kamakura. Before he found instruction in swordsmanship, if that's what he was looking for, he went to the Tsurugaoka Hachimangu shrine there.

Kagehisa's choice of this shrine was almost certainly no accident. The central Tsurugaoka Hachimangu shrine is dedicated to Hachiman, the Buddhist deity of war. Yoritomo Minamoto built the shrine in the twelfth century, immediately after his clan defeated the Taira family, securing for Yoritomo the position of shogun. The shrine was, when Kagehisa arrived, a vast complex of smaller temples and shrines, mixing worship of both Shinto and Buddhist ritual. Today, it is most famous as the site of annual displays of *yabusame*, or mounted archery, where horsemen ride down lanes, shooting at targets as they go, cheered by thousands.

When we read of famous warriors and swordsmen secreting themselves in temples and shrines, looking for divine inspiration in their art, we may have images of them standing alone out in a temple courtyard, swinging their weapons as ascetic priests in flowing robes glide gracefully by in the background. But places like Tsurugaoka were natural destinations for those of the samurai class. After losing their leader, or when the fortunes of war left their fiefs financially destitute, or often because they grew tired of the bloodshed and gore, many samurai became monks. While their ecclesiastical duties occupied some of their day, they did not necessarily abandon their martial arts training. In fact, maintaining combative skills at many temples and shrines would have been encouraged, since one never knew when the next insurrection or war could have posed a threat. While Kagehisa may have prayed for supernatural guidance and contemplated the Meaning of Life at Tsurugaoka, he was probably also watching or training with others who knew which end of the sword went where, to say the least.

According to documents detailing the foundation of Kagehisa's style of swordsmanship, he spent six days at the temple, and on the night of the last day, he was out alone in the yard, swinging his sword, when an attacker—similarly armed—slipped up behind him. The intent, goes the story, was robbery. (Are we callous skeptics for wondering just what kind of target an itinerant orphaned young man might have made for a robber? Possibly. On the other hand, given the poverty that afflicted so much of Japan during that era, it's possible Kagehisa might have been a tempting mark if for no other reason than to steal his weapon. Kagehisa's Bizen blade would have been worth more than the net income of most Japanese at that time.) As the assailant came just to within cutting distance, sword drawn and ready to strike, Kagehisa suddenly whirled around and slashed with his own weapon, killing the would-be attacker at the last possible moment.

Here's what I've always liked about Kagehisa. In most stories of this nature, the killing of the attacker would have meant a kind of instant enlightenment. "Having thus discovered the secrets of the sword, our founder created the blah-blah ryu," goes the refrain in many of the ancient *densho*, or scrolls of transmission. Not in the case of the Itto ryu. Kagehisa whacked out an assailant—and hadn't a clue as to how he'd done it. Rather than being lightning-struck with a sudden realization into the heart of swordsmanship, his first thought was to get out of Dodge, lest he be arrested for murder. (Which, to return to the position of the skeptic, makes us suspect Kagehisa was training with someone, things got out of hand, and the opponent was killed.) He went to Edo, the capitol city—a bustling place, and larger than London at that time. Kagehisa could find anonymity there, in case authorities were looking for him. He found a school of the sword as well. He entered the Kannemaki ryu, a school of the art taught by Kannemaki Jisai.

Kannemaki was an accomplished expert in the Chujo ryu, one of the oldest schools of swordsmanship in Japan, one that is regrettably extinct today. We know very little of its techniques or strategies. Kannemaki apparently knew a lot about them; he had mastered the system and had found some room for improvement—evidently enough to compel him to found his own, new school of swordsmanship, the Kannemaki ryu. He was thriving in Edo; he'd picked a good location and a better time to teach the art of the sword. Battlefield combat had been almost entirely replaced by one-on-one dueling or other such individual fighting. It was an atmosphere that led to an explosion of different techniques and systems, and Kannemaki had a long list of those eager to train with him. Kagehisa readily fit into the school. He must have trained hard and pleased his teacher, since he spent five years under Kannemaki's tutelage. And during that time, we can imagine, treating it as though it were some kind of Zen koan, he thought about that killing in the temple yard back at Tsurugaoka Hachimangu, wondering how it was he had struck at precisely the right moment.

Another glimpse of Kagehisa's character is revealed in what happened next. One day he approached Kannemaki, informing his teacher, "Okay, I've learned all you've got to teach me." It's possible Kagehisa was a bit more diplomatic than that. Formal Japanese is a language that allows one to be indirect and still get across the idea. Given Kagehisa's personality, it's a good bet he didn't use the more formal and gracious modes of speaking and made his point in the plain Japanese of the day, more or less as I've translated it. It is an equally good bet that Kannemaki's response was equally brusque. "Oh yeah? Show me." And that is how they ended up facing one another, teacher and student, wooden practice weapons in their fists.

It did not go well for Kannemaki. Not the first time, when Kagehisa's *bokken* deflected his strike and countered, landing lightly but with enough force to make Kagehisa's point. Nor the second, when Kannemaki demanded a rematch. He lost again. Kagehisa, it seems, had discovered the secret of his success over the assailant back at the temple.

I met a direct descendant of Kannemaki's once, in a dojo in Nagano Prefecture where he practiced iaido. He was somewhat surly and distant, and another member there told me it was because he just didn't like foreigners. I have always projected that descendant's personality on Kannemaki Jisai, which is not entirely fair, of course. To his credit, Kannemaki was gracious and honest enough to admit he'd been beaten. He asked Kagehisa how he'd done it.

"I did not think of winning in the contest," Kagehisa replied. "I concentrated only on not losing. It was with that kind of attitude that I waited for you to start your attack; then I allowed myself to react without any conscious thought."

The modern reader, if he knows anything of Japanese swordsmanship, is apt to pause here, noting some strategic discrepancies. Waiting for an attack is almost always a good idea when you can do it. In a one-on-one contest involving swords or most other weapons, the guy who moves first—unless he is very, very good— is likely to lose. There are instances, though, such as facing the threat of multiple opponents, when standing there and waiting for something to happen is not the way to succeed. So we have to be careful about taking Kagehisa's explanation too literally. It is better to assume he meant that by finding the right opportunity— whether by waiting in a passive sense or "encouraging" the opponent to move first in some way—a contest can be decided at the very last second by a single strike. And that a single strike, correctly understood and implemented, can crystallize a thousand techniques. This "one strike" strategy was the basis for Kagehisa's swordsmanship. In recognition of its fundamental importance, he gave himself a new name: Ito Ittosai Kagehisa. Kagehisa left Edo, traveling over much of central Japan during the last half of the sixteenth century. He engaged in practice duels with a number of swordsmen and other martial artists, none of whom bested him. It was a period of testing his theory of the "one sword," or *itto.*

Kagehisa gave instruction to scores of those wishing to train under him. His Itto ryu achieved a prominence in martial arts circles matched by few other styles of swordsmanship in the history of Japan. But in the truest sense of the word, he had only two who could have been considered his students.

Zenki was a commoner working a ferry that Kagehisa took across the Yodo River, in the southern part of Japan's main island. Legend has it that Zenki, even though not of samurai status, had longed all his life to be a swordsman. To achieve his goal, he made a habit of looking over the passengers on his ferry. If any looked as if they might be proficient in the art, his approach would be abrupt and to the point: "Wanna fight?" He would challenge them to a duel on the spot. It was a risky way to learn. Some samurai or others skilled in using a sword would have laughed him off; others might have politely declined. But his method was not all that different than walking into a dark and smoky biker bar today, sizing up the occupants, then sticking one's face into that of the toughest-looking among them and saying "Let's dance." You can learn a lot about combat doing that. You also risk gathering some impressive scars. Zenki used an auxiliary oar as a substitute bokken when he did get takers willing to duel with him, which gives an even clearer picture of the man's intent. Here's a guy so desperate to learn swordsmanship that he's using a spare oar against a live blade. How much he'd managed to learn by the time Kagehisa came on board his ferry we can't know. But it was not enough. Kagehisa took Zenki up on his challenge once the ferry had reached the far shore, and beat him convincingly. Zenki was intelligent enough to realize he was in the company of an extraordinary warrior. He fell to his knees and begged Kagehisa to take him on as a disciple. Kagehisa accepted.

The other of Kagehisa's direct students was Migogami Tenzen, a lower-ranked samurai of the Satomi clan, from Awa Province. Migogami was there to answer the ad Kagehisa posted while passing through a town, notifying any and all that he was seeking competition. He wished to test his Itto ryu against all comers. Tenzen was happy to oblige. And when he met the same fate as Zenki, he, too, asked to be taken on by Kagehisa to learn the secrets of the one-sword strike. The trio traveled together constantly. There is no record of Kagehisa ever establishing a headquarters or working permanently for a clan. Zenki and Tenzen learned a great deal more besides technique in this way. They had to adapt to constantly changing conditions. They were often hungry, always seen as strangers. They were susceptible to attacks from bandits who roamed most of the roads in Japan in those days, as well as from those who would have liked nothing better than to say they had killed the famous Kagehisa. Almost as trying would have been living with Kagehisa himself, who, by all accounts, was a cold fish, arrogant and inscrutable in his ways.

By 1588, Kagehisa was already well over fifty years old. He felt the time had come for him to choose a successor, the leader of the next generation of his Itto ryu. Several students had trained with him. Many of them were from other ryu and had gone on to incorporate principles of the Itto ryu into their systems. It was, even in its first generation, an enormously influential school of fencing. Still, of all these students, only Zenki and Tenzen were of the caliber Kagehisa considered worthy of inheriting the headmastery of his tradition. He also knew that the two were so evenly matched in their skills that the technical differences between them were slight, inconsequential. And so he devised another standard, a test for determining which of them would succeed him. It could not have come as a surprise to either that his test was a bizarre one.

The three were in Sahara. (No, not the desert in Africa—although that would make for an engaging story, wouldn't it?) No, Sahara was a small town in Shimofusa Province, where Kagehisa laid out the details of the test he proposed. "Since you are so evenly matched in your abilities, there is no way for me to make a judgment that would have any validity. Therefore," he said, "you will have to make the decision for me."

Tenzen and Zenki could have had no idea what it was their teacher proposed. Kagehisa explained it. "You will fight to decide who inherits the ryu," he said. "Whatever rules there are, you two come up with them between yourselves."

The two must have been incredulous. Even accustomed as they were to Kagehisa's eccentricities, this was extreme. They were fully aware that in a battle of the sort Kagehisa was proposing, there would only be one real way of determining a victor. The one who survived would be the winner. Tenzen and Zenki agreed to the use of *shinken*, or live, metal swords. The duel was to take place at dawn on the following day.

The site of the duel was a rolling meadow called Koganegahara that is still there, and still looks about the same as it must have on that early spring morning. There are copses of oaks on three sides. Their brown, withered leaves were still clinging to the branches. The sun would have been just striking the ground, sparkling the frozen dew, when the three arrived at the meadow, their footsteps crunching. Without a word, Kagehisa walked to the far edge of the field and sat on a rock. In front of him, he placed a warrior's *uchiwa*, a fan made of lacquered elm and tough, leathery paper. On top of the fan he placed one of his most treasured possessions, a sword he'd nicknamed "Ogre

Slayer." Beside the sword he put a scroll with the full transmission of the ryu written on it. Possession of the scroll was proof the owner was the rightful heir of the ryu.

Kagehisa folded his arms, waited. Zenki and Tenzen bowed in their teacher's direction. Nobody was taking notes for us to read centuries later, but we can imagine the scene. Zenki taking off a heavy overcoat *haori* and placing it carefully on the ground. Tenzen tying up the sleeves of his kimono with a strip of twisted paper string. When they had finished the rituals surrounding a duel, they took up their weapons and bowed to one another. Since Tenzen was junior to Zenki, having been accepted into Kagehisa's tutelage later, he may have bowed a bit lower. Zenki, perhaps misinterpreting this as a sign of emotional weakness on Tenzen's part, immediately raised his sword above his head. Tenzen, more cautious, kept his weapon low, the tip pointed directly at Zenki's throat.

It is very difficult for us to put ourselves in the place of men like this, to feel the tension they must have felt. In samurai movies, such one-on-one encounters are usually depicted as a kind of deadly ballet. Flashing swords, acrobatic movement, the slither and clang of metal struck. The reality was that in most battles of this nature, about 90 percent of the "action" was carried on in the minds of the participants. Movement was kept to an absolute minimum. The difference between living and dying was going to be measured by fractions of a second in timing or distancing. This would have been especially true in the case of these two swordsmen. The defining strategy of the Itto ryu, of course, was to wait for an opponent to make a move and then counter—or to force him, through posture or "attitude," to make the first move. Such a gambit, however, did not mean an opponent's initial move had to come in the form of an all-out attack. Often, all the Itto ryu swordsman needed or wanted was a slight shift in balance on the part of his opponent, a mere flickering of his sword's tip. A movement that might not, to an observer, look like much more than a twitch would provide the opening. Tenzen and Zenki were experts at discerning these. Their duel must have been carried on so subtly that to anyone unschooled in martial art, the temptation to start admiring the countryside, plan the evening's meal, or even to doze while waiting for something, anything, to happen, would have been significant. Those unfamiliar with the reality of this kind of close, personal combat, would likely be oblivious to the energy that was being expended before them.

The sun rose fully, drained of the dawn's angry red, taking on a bright yellow cast, a promise of the spring that was on its way. Dry, dead leaves rustled. The dew shimmered and vanished. And from the two contestants, nothing. Oh, maybe Zenki's forward foot would slide forward a few inches. Tenzen would pull his back an equal distance. A shifting from side to side, mirrored by the opponent. But there were no blows, no shouts, no slack between them.

Again, few of us can know what goes on in a man's mind in that kind of situation. So it is nothing but speculation to guess what it was that caused Zenki to do what he did next. Maybe he'd overestimated his own prowess. Maybe his impoverished background led him to be tempted, distracted even for a second or two, by the thought of all the fame that would come with the position of headmaster of such a renowned ryu. Maybe, way down deep inside him, there was a stray vein of fear that the contest had exposed. Whatever it was, Zenki broke. He leaped away from Tenzen, scrambling toward the edge of the field where Kagehisa sat watching. He ran directly for the scroll in front of Kagehisa, grabbed it, and turned, breaking in a sprint for the road.

Tenzen was after him, running to catch up, his sword still in his fist. He gained on Zenki, caught him at the edge of the field.

Zenki, sensing the pursuit, whipped around, putting the scroll between his teeth to free both hands. But he did not try to fight; he dropped his sword and snatched for the trunk of a sapling, pulling it over to put the limb between himself and Tenzen. Tenzen never paused. He raised his blade, then cut. The sword passed through the sapling as easily as it cut into muscle and bone. Zenki died on the spot, the scroll still in his mouth.

What happened after the duel between Tenzen and Zenki is well known in martial arts circles. Tenzen took a new name. He became Ono Taadaki and assumed the status of the second headmaster of the Itto ryu. He served as a fencing instructor to the first Tokugawa shogun, Ieyasu, and taught a number of swordsmen, some of whom went on to found their own martial ryu. As for Kagehisa, we know very little about him after he walked off the field at Koganegahara that frosty, late winter morning. There is a document that seems to indicate he took the tonsure and became a Buddhist monk. Another source reputes, however, that Kagehisa died not long after the duel between Zenki and Tenzen. Records from Shimofusa Province (now Chiba and Ibaraki Prefectures) note that someone with the same name died at the age of ninety-four there, though whether this is the same Kagehisa is unclear.

The mysterious end of Kagehisa's life is fitting, in a way. He was enigmatic, to say the least. He discovered a fundamental principle of swordsmanship but was able to pass it on to only two others, one of whom killed the other—at his instigation. He was a master, arguably without peer, in matters of technique. Yet he never seemed to penetrate, as so many other great swordsmen did, into the realms of the spiritual. Whether this was from a disinterest or a dispositional limitation on his part, we can never know. Was he satisfied, watching his two best students try to kill one another? Did he consider his life to be a success? Other sword masters have left their reflections in written form. Even the half-feral Musashi left a book that gives us some hints that he perceived a philosophical path to be the real destination of swordsmanship. But Kagehisa? His life might best be exemplified by that young man, standing in the dark in the middle of the temple grounds, a dead man at his feet, a bloody sword in his hand, and not the slightest idea of how it all happened or what it all meant.

3

Igen

Dignity

At first glance, a person's measure of dignity is manifested. There is a dignity in one's appearance. There is dignity in a calm demeanor. There is dignity in a paucity of words. There is dignity in the perfection of etiquette. There is dignity in reserved behavior. There is dignity in a penetrating insight and a clear perspective on matters. These are all reflected on the surface of the person. Ultimately, however, their foundation is in a simplicity of thought and a constant tautness of spirit.

—Yamamoto Tsunetomo, *Hagakure*

It was midsummer. Hot and humid, even more so there under the eaves. I was up in the attic of the old garage at the house my sensei was renting, crouched down to avoid the nail-spiked beams that stabbed or raked my head every time I straightened. Since I was around, he decided it was time to get to the chore he'd put off too long: moving a whole raft of dusty boxes and assorted junk that had belonged to a previous tenant. Sensei wanted to store some of his own boxes and junk up there, so we were hauling down the clutter so it could be stacked at the curb to be taken away. The air in the attic was thick and stifling. Lazy strands of cobwebs swirled around whenever I moved. I ducked a couple of times when I heard the drone of wasps that had built mud-daubed nests up in the rafters and were irritated at my company. To pass the time during this sweaty chore, I started to ask Sensei about various ways of saying things in Japanese. I was working on verbs.

"How do you say 'to sleep,' Sensei?" I peered down at him through the trapdoor in the garage ceiling where he was stacking some boxes of Christmas tree ornaments, many of them broken if the sounds they were making were a reliable indicator.

"*Nemuru*," came his reply, muffled a little as he bent over to rearrange another pile of boxes that were starting to slide.

"How about 'to count'?"

"*Kazoeru.*"

This went on for some time. Sensei's answers were distracted; he was beginning to realize just how much stuff was up in this space. Space on the floor of the garage, which hadn't been plentiful when we began, was rapidly diminishing.

"How about 'to spit'?" I was hanging halfway through the hole, passing him another box. It felt like someone's brick collection inside.

"I don't know," he said.

I blinked.

"I don't know that word," he said, "because polite people do not *use* that word."

Several years after my sensei had returned to Japan, I followed, to visit him. One of his neighbors was talking with me one day, and when I told him of that exchange—about how my sensei said he didn't use words he considered impolite—the neighbor nodded and said, "Yep, he's a *bandomusha*." I didn't know the word. The neighbor explained that bandomusha was used to describe someone of civility; someone with a sense of propriety, who carried and conducted themselves with dignity. It was a good word to add to my limited Japanese vocabulary, I thought, and I did.

Later on, however, in other parts of Japan, people looked at me quizzically when I used it, so I looked it up in a Japanese dictionary. The definition explained that it was a word unique to the Kinki region of Japan (which includes the cities of Nara and Kyoto). It was also archaic. Bandomusha was a word that referred to a samurai or a member of the warrior caste, a word confined in usage to that area of Japan and to the feudal period. Later, consulting with several knowledgeable Japanese speakers in Japan, both natives and foreigners, this is the same definition I got.

It wasn't until I returned to Japan and went back to my teacher's house that I had a chance to ask about why the neighbor had used it as he had. Turns out bandomusha is one of those colloquial terms one encounters in Japan in rural areas. They are words that are either unique, or that are standard Japanese but have, over the generations, taken on a special or non-standard definition in some small towns or villages. Yes, my sensei explained, the dictionary definition is correct. But in the little area where he lived—an area consisting of no more than a few thousand people—the term *bandomusha*, somewhere back during the pre-modern days, had acquired the additional connotation of a person with dignity.

It's too bad the connotation never achieved wider acceptance. There may be another word in standard Japanese that approximates it, but I don't know what it would be. I don't even know a good equivalent in English. Maybe "gentleman" might once have sufficed. We might say of someone that he or she "has class." To call someone "dignified" seems, well, a trifle old-fashioned, doesn't it? Too bad. Just as *bandomusha*—in the sense it is used in my sensei's part of Japan—could be used more often, we ought to consider using the word *dignity* more readily in our conversations.

I recalled that summer afternoon when Sensei and I cleaned the garage attic some time later, when I read the biography of Gichin Funakoshi. The grandson of the founder of modern karate recalled that Funakoshi had refused, no matter how much the grandson tried to get him to say it, to utter the word *socks*. Even in his own home, Funakoshi considered the word impolite and vulgar, and so would always call socks "these." Sure, it's a little odd from our perspective, where footwear does not seem especially, well, unseemly. But such were Funakoshi's standards. And he stuck to them. Not long ago, I read an interview with Moriteru Uyeshiba, the grandson of aikido's founder, Morihei Uyeshiba. He remarked that his grandfather normally had a composed demeanor, but would become angry in an eyeblink when one of his students neglected a matter of etiquette or committed some breach of conduct in behavior, no matter how apparently insignificant.

It is easy to dismiss these parts of the characters of Funakoshi and Uyeshiba as eccentricities. It's also easy to read too much into their habits. Like many other famous figures in martial arts, particularly those who lived in the past century (and consequently, about whom comparatively much is known, and there are still people alive who knew them and trained with them), we can go overboard. We read into some aspect of their character, or even some isolated incident reported by one of their followers, some meaning that is blown far out of proportion. If Master Suzuki liked tuna fish sandwiches, we impart to this something of cosmic import and profundity and incorporate a sandwich-making ritual into our training. If Master Ohara disliked hot baths, we infer that making our daily ablutions in tepid water will reveal the Meaning of Life. Funakoshi and Uyeshiba were odd ducks. They were both countrified—Funakoshi from the backwaters of Okinawa, and Uyeshiba a hick from Kii Province, which is now part of Wakayama Prefecture. So some of their behavior and habits may simply be nothing more meaningful than the Appalachian hillbilly's penchant for eating peas with his knife. But I think that viewed through the overall perspective of their lives, these predilections of Uyeshiba and Funakoshi reveal a sense of propriety, a natural, unaffected result of a lifetime devoted to becoming a person of quality. A person, as they'd say from where my sensei hails, who deserves to be called a bandomusha.

In Funakoshi's vocabulary, he might have used the word *tanme*. It's from the Ryukyuan language, used to describe a well-bred person. From the region around where Uyeshiba was raised, they may have used the expression *ikki-tosen*: "one man who is worth a thousand." No matter how they thought of it, however, Funakoshi and Uyeshiba and so many other great masters of the martial arts and Ways have shown a regard for decorum. They seem to have tried, though not always successfully, to inculcate in themselves and in their students, a sense of *igen*: dignity.

Nobody who knows anything about life in feudal Japan places a lot of value on the words of Yamamoto Tsunetomo, the author of the *Hagakure*. Often cited as a classic on the noble code of the samurai, his eighteenth-century memoirs/analects are, more objectively viewed and placed in historical context, often rambling, contradictory, and almost absurdly romantic. (Although, come to think of it, my own work has been similarly characterized.) Yamamoto was a lot more like Don Quixote than he was a reflection of the best of Japan's warrior class.

Reading him, he always reminds me of Cervantes' slightly addled crackpot, prattling on and on to his erstwhile manservant about chivalry and the glories of the past. (Yamamoto's version of Sancho Panza was Tsuramoto Tashiro, a young samurai who for some reason had lost his job as a recorder of deeds and documents. Tsuramoto began visiting Yamamoto when the latter was living in partial seclusion, near the Saga fortress in Kyushu, and began recording Yamamoto's often stream-of-consciousness discourses, a text that eventually became the *Hagakure*.) In the case of his comments on dignity, though, quoted at the beginning of this chapter, Yamamoto has some revealing commentary on the nature of it. He observes that for some, dignity is made evident through appearance. If you have ever seen an army general in full regalia, you have seen this attempt at manifesting dignity. The stiff, high-peaked hat, the chest full of medals, epaulets that make his shoulders look broad; all the aspects of the general's uniform are meant, consciously or subconsciously, to convey the appearance of dignity and power.

Many a would-be master of the martial arts follows this route of adopting appurtenance to try to achieve a semblance of dignity. Have you seen the getups, gewgaws, fripperies, and frills sported by some of these souls? Uniforms are bedecked with so many patches, they resemble the cowling of an Indy race car. My favorites are those who feel compelled to sew patches reading SENSEI or MASTER on their bosoms or shoulders, just in case someone might walk into the place and overlook them or their exalted status. Belts are embroidered with names and *kanji* and hash marks to denote something or other. Others try to attain some measure of dignity by adopting mannerisms they think might give them that status. Most who have spent any time at all in a karate dojo will be familiar with the renowned "karate strut." It is an exaggerated swagger, something more like a waddle in the unfortunately frequent cases where the masters are packing a little more padding around the midsection than would appear seemly in a Trained Killer. More often, though, you will see the karate strut in young, recently promoted black belts. It is an aggressive stride, making them look faintly ridiculous from the point of view of someone who actually knows something about the kinetics of martial art. From their own side of things, however, the strut reminds them very much of the stride of Toshiro Mifune in one of his samurai movies, and they are ever so pleased with the effect it creates.

Indeed, such efforts at attaining dignity through one's superficial appearance might gain some admiration from those who are impressed by such things. But like all that is apparent on the surface and consequently apt to be shallow, these expressions meant to convey dignity are mostly illusion. They have little to do with real igen. These examples—of what igen is *not*—come readily to mind. That's because it is easier to describe the lack of dignity (is it because we see so much more of it?) than to explain what it is. True dignity of the sort one sees emerging from a serious study of the budo, or any other art, comes from deep within and is brought to the surface over time. It comes from a sense of humility, in part. And in part, I suspect, it comes from respecting oneself.

Self-respect is not to be confused with self-esteem, at least not as that latter expression has come to be used in popular culture. Self-esteem has become a vague phrase to describe something that, had they more of it, muggers would not bash in skulls for monetary rewards insufficient to purchase a taco platter; students would perform better on their SATs than opossums taking the same test; and boys and girls too young to legally vote would find more productive uses of their time and energy than in spawning bastard offspring. No, self-esteem refers to what we think of ourselves. Hitler had excellent self-esteem. So does a successful bank robber. Self-respect, on the other hand, is the notion that we have value and worth to the extent that we have earned it. We earn self-respect by gaining the respect of others. As Clyde Kimura, a fellow judoka who has taught the art to hundreds of university students, used to say, "You can't respect yourself until you learn to respect others." From this perspective, the dignity that comes from self-respect comes by a deserved elevation of our own character. In a wider sense, behaving with igen serves the dual purpose of making ourselves better and regulating our conduct. Dignity—true dignity—is a kind of moral sense.

To link dignity with morality may seem odd—especially when we do so in the context of dignity in the budo. I have been writing for martial arts publications for more than two decades, and in all that time, I can never remember seeing any articles that were devoted to morality. That is probably because it is a touchy and problematic topic. After all, there are practitioners of karate-do, judo, aikido, and so on, who come from every religious and philosophical background. Morality, expressed in a code of "this is right and that is wrong," might be construed as narrow-minded and authoritarian. And to some extent, that is true. Just because I am a seventh-degree black belt in kendo does not give me the status or position to tell you whether it is morally wrong to divorce or gamble. There is nothing in any of the *dojo kun*— the prescripts outlining the basic tenets of a particular system or budo—that covers the morality of abortion. A uniform morality or set of moral standards, in fact, would be particularly harsh for many budoka to accept, because one of the primary goals of the budo is for each practitioner to discover his own answers about life. Budo isn't a cult. It is a platform for the individual to reach out and find and perfect what is important to him or her. That is not to say, however, that virtually any kind of behavior should be accepted by the budoka—not his own behavior nor that of others. Just because we don't impose a specific morality in the dojo does not mean we should suspend all judgments about what is good and bad in the world.

Granted, it is difficult to make that distinction sometimes—especially when a lot of the people we have looked to as exemplars of the good way are revealed to be such scoundrels. Sports figures, political figures, even religious leaders are exposed on a near-daily basis as louts, cheats, and miscreants. If we are fortunate, our parents provided models when we were young. So did teachers and other responsible adults, who guided us in shaping our own morality. Sadly, many who train in various budo cannot always, or even often, rely on senior martial arts exponents to serve in the same capacity. At a national-level karate tournament a few years ago, a young black belt (young, but old enough to know better)—unquestionably one of the most promising champions of his generation—got drunk one evening after the competition. With the aid of equally drunken teammates, he proceeded to trash his hotel room to the tune of several thousand dollars in damages. Tawdry, even illegal episodes of the Highly Ranked Master using the aura of his fame to seduce female students under his instruction are common. The same Masters, visiting at dojos to conduct seminars, routinely make overtures to women students in attendance, sometimes subtly, sometimes with all the light touch of an eighteen-wheeler coming down the road in fifth gear. These are the people we're supposed to emulate or to point to when it comes time to identify role models?

Of course, the argument is made that such antics are not exactly immoral in every instance or in everyone's estimation. There can be extenuating circumstances, all kinds of rationalizations that could be hauled out to defend them. And anyway,

Right Reverend Dave, why don't you get back on track here? You started out by talking about igen or dignity, or whatever it is. And now you're preaching a sermon on morality. What's the connection? Here it is: While such behavior might be defended on a variety of grounds, what is indefensible and what must matter to every serious budoka is that these kinds of actions are undignified. They *might* be judged stupid or in poor taste or immoral or criminal. They arguably lack a concern for others who might be injured or embarrassed by them. They possibly flaunt a disregard for individual conduct that is at odds with all the values perpetuated by the budo. For damned sure, however, they lack dignity. In short, while we may be able to forgive or explain or rationalize or excuse ourselves or our fellow budoka, we cannot deny their lack of dignity.

No matter our religious or moral belief system, in this maddeningly complicated world there will be all manner of decisions and actions we have to take that can be tough and difficult. Many situations present a variety of complexities, and trying to determine what's best can be like groping one's way through a cave. An old rock-climbing partner of mine, faced with such problems, used to employ what he modestly named, after himself, Hart's Maxim. "We don't always know what's *best* for us," he said. "But we usually know what's *right* for us." The budoka might have a slightly altered version of this when it comes to his own conduct. We may not know what kind of behavior is ultimately best for us. But if we have trained seriously in the budo and understand its ethos and traditions, we usually know which course has dignity and which one does not. Using igen as a compass cannot guarantee we'll always do the right thing; however, dignity—the sense of respect we have for ourselves engendered through a respect for others—is a powerful indicator of sincerity and propriety.

This is where we see igen and morality merge. It is also where the serious budoka can see that there is considerable strength in the culturing of igen. There can be no goal more important to the martial artist—not if he seeks to take his training beyond the limited range of physical technique and into a realm where the strategies of the budo become a reflection of the strategies one adopts in everyday life. Kofujita Yayoe, a master swordsman of the Yuishin Itto ryu, made that point eloquently, noting that strength and dignity are not very different at all, whether the "enemy" we face is an opponent in a fight or the uncertainties of life that confront us on a daily basis. Kofujita wrote:

> Whatever the circumstances, dignity does not change. Preparing correctly and boldly, not yielding to the enemy's movements—this is dignity. With this strategy, an enemy can be controlled without even moving. Overwhelming the opponent with one's own movement is strength. Within the calmness of a dignified bearing are hidden a thousand changes. Those movements that come from such a bearing have the power to deal with ten thousand changes that might appear. In essence, then, dignity and strength are the same.

4

Nakaima

The Eternal Present

Do not worship great men of the past. Seek instead
to follow in their accomplishments.

—Basho

Our sandals change but our journey continues on
the same.

—Okakura Kakuzo

The other day I was visiting at a friend's house, a woman who
is a *yudansha*, or black-belt holder, in a Japanese karate organization. She had, in fact, just received her certificate for the
rank of *nidan*, the second level of the black-belt ranks. I was curious to see if she had it on display. I was happy to see that she
did not. It is an unfortunate trend among many modern budoka
that evidence of rank is automatically assumed to be worthy of
hanging on the wall or put up in some other manner of presen-
tation. I know at least three non-Japanese men who have been

granted full licenses of mastery in classical Japanese *koryu* (the martial arts that still remain from the feudal period), and at least that many women who have been given licenses of nearly similar stature in *ikebana* (flower arranging), and at least twice as many men and women who have been granted similar papers or licenses in *chado*, the art of the tea ceremony. I am happy to say that none of them has any of these licenses or scrolls displayed in their homes. They are modestly tucked away, as they should be.

I did notice that in the home of the karate yudansha, she had the envelope holding the certificate sitting up on the mantelpiece of her apartment's fireplace. It was sitting in front of a picture, crackled and creased with age, of a man she told me was her grandfather. He was a stern, hard-looking piece of work, even as a youth, in this portrait that was made around the turn of the nineteenth century when he was posing for his college graduation ceremony. The old portrait and the certificate sitting in front of it may have been merely coincidental. I didn't ask the woman. I preferred to think it had not been; that it was, instead, a way of putting the certificate out in front of the photo of her ancestor, as such things are done in front of Shinto shrines or Buddhist *butsuden* in private homes in Japan. Report cards, letters, or other important documents are sometimes laid on or near these altars which contain the spirits of family ancestors, according to Shinto and Buddhist theology. Placing such objects close by is a way of bringing them to the attention of those who have departed but are still around in spirit. My own religious beliefs preclude ancestor worship. There is no doubt, however, that I indulge in ancestor veneration. For anyone involved in the classical martial art traditions of Japan, with their long lineages and rich histories, "the past," as Hawthorne wrote, "is always with us." Such regard for previous generations and for the things they valued and handed down to us may have a particular word in

Japanese to describe it. The best one I have encountered is one I suspect was borrowed and given a new twist in meaning by the late author and martial arts authority, Donn Draeger. He called it *nakaima*, which he interpreted as "the eternal present."

I have never heard or read the word nakaima apart from its mention in one of Draeger's books. When I consulted some Japanese language scholars about it, they told me it came from Shinto doctrine. "In the middle of now," is a poor translation; the concept is subtler. Nakaima, the language authorities explained, is the sense that each moment has value. As Draeger used it, nakaima is something like that, though a more precise definition, if I am reading him correctly, would be the Latin, *nunc et semper:* "as it was and evermore shall be." I think he used the word to describe the sense of timelessness, the intimate connection with the past felt by the practitioner of Japan's traditional arts. The connection is literal in some ways. Walk into a dojo in Japan or out into some field or yard where classical martial training is being conducted, and there are few clues that you are in the twenty-first century and not in the seventeenth. The dress is the same, the weapons are the same; the movements are no different if the transmission within the ryu has been honest and true. The connection is also on a spiritual level. We are linked with the past on more than just a physical level when we train.

When I think of nakaima as I believe Draeger was using the word, I often think of Abe Shosaburo. I never met him. He'd been dead more than twenty years before I began training. For me, his presence had been felt entirely through some old photographs and stories my sensei had shared with me. The first time I visited Japan I went to his grave. I stood in front of it after lighting incense, and thought about who he had been and how his life had touched mine, half a world away. We were connected, through nakaima.

Abe was one of that hardy group who maintained the traditions of classical Japanese martial arts in the years before WWII. From images that remain, they did not look like a particularly fun bunch of people. He did joke, I know. Sensei told me Abe would often laugh about his "illustrious" samurai heritage, noting that in hundreds of years, while his family had never distinguished themselves, they'd never suffered any terrible misfortunes, either. "We were more careful about who we *didn't* fight than who we did," he told my sensei.

Little evidence of his wit was obvious in the photographs I saw. Doubtless that's due in part to the nature of photography in those days. Most pictures taken, especially in the more rural areas like where Abe lived, were formal portraits and meant to be serious matters. Abe looks out from a sepia image, lips tight, gaze steely, and while he's wearing Western clothes, he does not look comfortable in them. Abe saw men die under a sword. He was alive back in the days when disputes and political disagreements were still settled with duels. He had seen, he'd told my teacher, two men hack one another to death on a street in Nara. He was the last person in our lineage to have seen a sword used to its most practical ends, and I believe that's why it was a different weapon in his hands than it could ever be in mine. So possibly that accounts for the expression on his face.

But I know too, that much of his personality was shaped by a fervent desire to maintain the martial tradition he had inherited. He was an expert swordsman of one branch of the Yagyu Shinkage ryu. That did not mean he was feudal in his outlook. In the early part of the twentieth century, Abe was also keenly interested in Japanese national politics and their successful modernization. He was a member of a local committee that built schools for children who had, in traditional Japan, been excluded from formal education unless they were of the upper classes. He preferred whiskey to sake. Nevertheless, he told my teacher again and again that Japan would succeed in the modern world only if it kept polished the culture of its past.

Abe made his living buying silk for kimono makers in and around Osaka. He traveled over much of southern Japan as part of his job, and so he had a chance to talk with people and to observe what was going on in Japan as that nation built itself into a military power. He was not in favor of such a path. This might surprise some readers who would assume that, being a descendant of the samurai, men like Abe would have been jingoistic, emperor-worshipping hawks. The truth is that most of the more educated descendants of the upper classes of old Japan, including the samurai caste, had an antipathy for the modern conscript army there. Plenty of them were enthusiastic about Japan becoming a military power, but they tended to serve in Japan's navy, which had a distinctly aristocratic air about it.

Abe, however, was part of the contingent that believed all of Japan's post-feudal military was, at best, a flock of poseurs manipulated by business and industrial leaders. I know, I know. If you talk to Japanese today, they will all tell you their parents or grandparents or great-grandparents were passionately opposed to the war. If all of them are telling the unvarnished truth, it's hard to imagine how Japan mustered a military to begin the war. In Abe's case, though, we have letters he wrote to relatives, detailing his opposition. He wrote a letter right after the war started, describing it as a "haggling of merchants grabbing for their share of profits in the world's marketplace." About a year after the war began, even though it was at that time proceeding well for the Japanese, the bottom was falling out of the silk industry. What was being manufactured went into supplies for the war, not kimono. A bout with rheumatic fever in his childhood had left him exempt from the draft, yet even so, he could not make a living buying silk. Abe sold his house in Osaka and returned to the countryside where he'd been born. He farmed, and trained with his sword, teaching the art to the young man who would later be my sensei.

It was my teacher, still in high school at that time, who went to Abe's house to tell him news that had just come over the radio. Some kind of completely new bomb had been dropped over Hiroshima, some kind of super-fire bomb, the radio said, that had caused destruction of a sort never seen before. Abe and my teacher were interrupted when a car pulled up on the road below the house. Two men, prefectural government officials, had come to see Abe. My teacher told me years later that it was the most frightened the teacher had been during the entire war. Such officials did not come to make social calls. They did not come to bring good news. Japan during the war was for all purposes a police state. If you spoke out against the war, if you were not enthusiastic enough *for* the war, chances were very good that an informer, a neighbor or even someone from your own family, would make a report of it to the local authorities. Civilians were routinely called into police stations for questioning, and sometimes worse. Abe was, by all accounts, a brave man. But he was also circumspect. He'd kept his opinions about the war strictly to himself and to members of his immediate family. My sensei told me that Abe did not even discuss it much with him. And while neither Abe nor my sensei had any idea what these two wanted, they were certain it did not bode well.

Even before the bombing of Hiroshima, the conditions in Japan were awful, and getting worse by the week. Food shortages, power outages, a lack of nearly everything had combined with almost constant losses on the battlefield, and by 1945, Japan was a desperate place. In light of the crisis, the government engaged in frantic propaganda, warning that if foreigners did manage to invade the homeland, that rape, looting, and unimaginable violence would be unleashed. In response, civilians were told they must defend their country to the very last man, woman, and child, if necessary. In many places, they began to drill with the only practical weapons still at hand. They sharpened bamboo poles. They formed into militias, practicing to make what would be suicidal charges against the feared invaders. That is why the government officials had come to Abe. They knew he was a martial artist. They wanted him to organize the people in the town nearby and teach them how to fight with the makeshift bamboo spears.

It isn't hard to understand Abe's dilemma. He knew that training old men and housewives and schoolchildren to charge into a fight against a professional army—bamboo spears against automatic weapons—was stupid and futile, and would do nothing but temporarily prolong a war he was against. On the other hand, the prefectural officials were not exactly "asking." Their request amounted to an order. Refusing it was unthinkable. People had disappeared, hauled off by police never to be seen again, for much less than turning down an order to train the citizenry to fight the expected invaders. Sensei told me that standing there beside Abe, he had not even breathed, waiting to see what Abe would do. He said Abe looked off toward the crest of a ridge of hills, sucked in his breath at last, and in polite language said he did not think such a plan would be feasible. He didn't flat-out refuse. He couched his response in a way that said "no" without saying "nope," a distinction possible given the labyrinthine construction of the Japanese language. The junior official actually took a step back when he heard this. The senior, however, gave Abe a long, hard look. And said nothing at all. Then both got back in their car and drove away. They were not high up enough to actually arrest him. But they would be talking before the day was out, Abe knew, with those who could and would.

Abe's joke about his ancestors' prowess in knowing who not to fight being more important than the enemies and battles one did pick must have been more than just self-deprecating humor. Abe had inherited something of their talent, or so it seemed. Within a few days, another "super-fire bomb" was dropped, this time at Nagasaki. Prefectural police and other government agency workers obviously had more important matters on their hands than some obstreperous country bumpkin who didn't want to teach spearmanship. Japan's surrender came shortly thereafter. My sensei later discovered that arrest warrants had actually been written out for Abe, but were never delivered. Had they been, and had Abe been arrested, it's a good bet he'd have ended up out on some remote Nara hillside with a bullet in his head. It was as close a brush with death as he'd ever had, and both he and his student knew it.

"What were you thinking when you said 'no'?" my sensei asked him, after the war was over.

"I was terrified," Abe said, matter-of-factly. "Didn't know if I was going to keep from crapping in my pants I was so scared." He explained, "I didn't want to die, and when I was thinking about that, thinking about myself, I was shaking. So I thought instead about my old teacher and his teacher and all the ancestors in our family. And that gave me the courage to do what I thought was right. I quit thinking about myself," Abe said, "and I thought about where I came from."

Since the sixties, at least, "finding oneself" has become almost an institution in our culture. We travel to ashram, to Buddhist temples, to Tibetan monasteries. We sit naked in the woods beating drums, crawl into American Indian sweat lodges, endure regimens designed to reveal our past lives, consult the *I Ching*, the Kabbalah, and the Book of the Dead. If there is a form of meditation in which we have not dabbled, it is only because our local community center has not yet offered it. If there is some kind of psychological therapy in which we have not enrolled, it is only because we cannot—at the moment, at least—afford it. At the root of all these exercises and endeavors is the urge to find out who we really are, to get at the heart of what we are all about. It all seems a trifle silly sometimes. Fat, self-absorbed Westerners dabbling in the esoteries of the East, or being guided by mystic time travel agents back to our incarnation as Egyptian royalty, or paying our therapists what amounts to a royal ransom for listening to our petty grievances and inner frailties. A more optimistic view would be that we have so completely conquered the necessities of life—making a living, healing or preventing disease, keeping the wild animals from knocking down our doors—that we can afford to indulge in these quests.

Regardless, it is obvious that many budoka are, as part of their training, off on their own search to find themselves. Those who are serious about their martial art training, however, have one big advantage over other seekers. We know that much of the answer lies not in asking "Who am I?", but rather in discovering "From where have I come?" The budoka, through his allegiance to a ryu, a dojo, or an art, recognizes that his life is part of a very long chain that has stretched far back into the past, and one that will continue—partially due to his own diligence and effort—well into the future. In this sense, the perspective of his existence is not entirely a self-centered one. It is a link in the chain, one small part of the "eternal present" of nakaima. And as Abe proved during his moment of crisis, the budoka always has available to him the strength of that chain to pull him through.

When I began training in the martial arts, I expected my sensei to ask a lot of questions about me. Why did I want to do this? I was surprised when among the first matters my sensei asked me about was—of all things—my grandmothers. When I'd gotten to know him better, I asked him why he'd taken such a tack in assessing me. "I wanted to see what kind of martial artist you'd make," he said. "I wanted to see if you would be able to contribute to the ryu. The best way to know about that was to know where you came from."

That response to my question was not exactly a revelation for me. I had been raised with a pervading sense of history—the history of the places I lived, my family, my country. Still, it caused me to think more deeply about budo and my place in it. I remember a *Peanuts* comic strip from about that same time where Lucy and her brother Linus were out looking up at the stars. Linus comments that looking out into the vast expanse of space made him feel "small and insignificant." Replied the caustic Lucy, "That's because you *are* small and insignificant." That might be overstating things. Nevertheless, it is important for us to understand that within our chosen budo, as within life itself, we are not at the pinnacle of things. We are a link in the chain. This is a mistake modern people can easily make today. We often lack a good historical perspective. Statistics are frequently cited, showing how few students know in which century the American Civil War occurred, or who the Allies were in the Second World War. While the popularity of genealogical research has soared recently, it is still common for people not to know from which country their great-grandparents came, or anything about them at all. Without a framework of history, we begin to accept the notion that nothing before or after us could be quite so worthy or interesting or valuable as we are right now. We're tempted to believe the illusion that we somehow sprang up without any sort of precedent. We ignore the fact that our existence, whether we acknowledge it or not, makes us a part of what has come from the past, and no matter who we are, we will have some influence over what happens long after we are gone.

I do not mean to imply that our pasts are necessarily remarkable or history making. Most of us have pedestrian pedigrees, to say the least. In my own case, I suppose my grandmothers, for instance, were not too different from those of most readers. One came from the rolling Kansas prairie, the other from a small town in Nova Scotia. Neither had much schooling or travel experience or material possessions. But both were honest and hardworking, and they put a lot of stock in such accomplishments and in other things like love and sincerity. Both endured their share of unhappiness and hard times, epidemics, unemployment, the joy of raising children, and the sweetness of success, however small or moderately measured. They made it through one of the world's greatest economic depressions and a couple of World Wars. They survived and produced another generation, and I am the product of that.

The same can be said, for the most part, of my ancestors in the martial ryu to which I belong. My teacher's teacher laughed about how little his predecessors had done in terms of being "great samurai warriors." But he wasn't kidding. They managed to avoid most of the major battles of Japan's long civil war. They didn't win any renowned duels or engage in heroic acts of valor. They were, in addition to their duties as samurai, usually engineers, overseeing road and dike construction in Owari Province. Yes, I am descended from warriors. But they were nerd warriors, probably with the feudal Japanese equivalent of a pocket protector stuck in their kimono. My teacher has some detailed accounts of their lives, how much they made in terms of the bushels of rice that served as salaries in those days, legal contracts they made. It isn't the stuff of great novels, let me tell you. Even so, to look over the details of their lives, to visit their graves, to hold the weapons they held and used—these are moments when I can feel the sense of nakaima. They are reminders that those of us engaged in the traditional disciplines of Japan are all a part of something much larger than ourselves. Something that goes back far and very deep and which is not composed only of dry history, of words on a page or relics, but the flesh and blood and sweat of people who are just like us. We are sustained through nakaima. Their sacrifices and contributions built a steady foundation for us to stand upon, one constructed of knowledge and experience. We stand on it whenever we practice the techniques and kata left to us. We understand through the process of nakaima that who we are has a great deal to do with where we came from; and from nakaima is imparted a sense of humility and gratitude and obligation for those who have gone before, along with a sense of responsibility for those who will follow after us.

It has become common for martial arts enthusiasts to study for a time several different methods of combat and to come up with their own "styles." These hybrid forms may well have some advantages, taking the best, allegedly, from this school or that art. They could arguably have some effectiveness as a form of self-defense or for physical training. I feel sorry for the individuals who undertake this kind of construction, however. I feel even sorrier for their students. They may be able to fight well. They may be in great shape. But they will never have the sources of emotional strength the traditional budoka has. That's because their hybrid concoctions have no nakaima. They live in a very limited present, one measured only by their own standards, one I suspect will pass all too quickly, handed down or carried on by no one. In terms of their art, they are alone in the worst sense of the word.

I know the story about Abe Shosaburo, his encounter with the officials at the end of the war, because his student, who was to become my teacher, was standing beside him when it happened. His experience is a part of me. His mannerisms, his particular way of doing the kata, his knowledge; some of these have been passed down to me. Also passed down was a tea bowl that had been given to Abe by his chado teacher. I keep it wrapped and put away along with other mementos, including a photo of my great-grandfather, a man with a ridiculously enormous handlebar moustache who is standing next to the first fire engine in the state of Kansas. Although they were both farmers more than once in their lives, Abe and my great-grandfather came from two almost completely different worlds. Even if they'd met, they could not have spoken a single word to one another. But while they had no idea they were doing it, they were working together in their lives to produce me, to make me what I am. The next time you practice your kata or bow in front of a shrine in a dojo dedicated to some long-ago master, you might want to think about your own links of this nature. And about those who have forged all the ones before it, and how you will do the same for those who will come after you. That is what nakaima is all about.

5

A Matter of Bathrobes . . .

This is about the connection between bathrobes and budo. Trust me.

During the late fall, flocks of robins gather in our yard, assembling for the long journey south, replaced almost immediately by flocks of a similar number of catalogs that appear in our mailbox. They are the harbingers of the coming holiday season. The catalogs tend to attract my attention in more or less direct inverse proportion to the amount of clothing worn by the female models on the cover. One that came last November, however, caught my eye in spite of the fact it did not appear to be advertising garments of the sort that would have, say, three-quarters of a century ago, had the publication confiscated and banned in about a minute. It was from a company providing all manner of Japanese furnishing and clothing, aimed at American consumers. *Tatami* mats, *shoji* screens, Japanese-style saws. In their clothing line, they carried *yukata*.

Yukata are sometimes mistaken for kimono by those who have little experience with things Japanese. The cut is loosely the same. A robe of floor length, with long lapels that fold over

Dave Lowry

and wide sleeves, they are the Japanese version of the bathrobe. Yukata is written with the characters that combine "hot water" with *kata.* Yes, the same kata, the same word used by those who practice the prearranged forms of karate and most other martial arts and Ways. In a roundabout way, it means "the shape useful for using around hot water." Japanese—this is a good example—is not always precise. Yukata are made of light cotton for summer wear; other heavier, padded materials are used for the versions worn in the winter months. Either way, they are nearly the perfect apparel for relaxing after a hot bath. In resorts all over Japan, you can see people out strolling on summer evenings, wearing yukata. Inns and many hotels leave clean, pressed yukata in guests' rooms. They are the most informal garment worn in Japan. *Bon odori,* the community dances held in honor of departed souls that take place at the end of the summer, would be unthinkable without the brightly patterned yukata, their designs swirling in the night as dancers snake and weave in the traditional spiraling steps. Even if you are at home, yukata are wonderful to slip into, for luxuriating in that sensation the Japanese call *sawayaka*—the warm, refreshing feeling that tingles and relaxes after soaking in a hot tub.

According to the catalog, the women's yukata offered for sale were American-made. They had been "redesigned to be more practical for modern women." Uh-oh. It has been my experience that whenever anything is "redesigned," we are all the worse for it. Remember the redesigning of Coke? Remember back before blister packaging, when you did not need a scalpel and a hacksaw to break into a pack of batteries? They redesigned the way our phone bill is configured, and I am convinced I am now paying the bill for a family of seven somewhere in Peru who make daily calls to Moscow. But I was curious.

How could something as simple as a yukata be redesigned? So I called the company and asked them about it.

"We made the sleeves narrower so they wouldn't be dragging across a table every time a woman reaches for something," I was told. "And we got rid of the vent under the arms."

"Oh really? Did you know what that vent was for, by the way?" I asked.

"Uhh . . . There was a reason for that?"

Yes, there is. To understand why yukata had vents under each arm, one must know something about traditional concepts of feminine beauty in old Japan. If you read the literature of ancient Japan that deals with this subject—it is convenient that the most famous novel of early Japan (and what is considered as well to be the first novel written anywhere), *Genji Monogatari*, was written by a woman—you will find numerous references to the beauty of a woman's torso. An exposed underarm and the flank of the breast were considered to be an especially beautiful and attractive aspect of a woman's body. Like cleavage is for us, these areas had a decidedly erotic appeal. We also know, from paintings, and later on, from prints of those eras, and from texts relating to feminine etiquette, that certain gestures were thought to make women look more attractive. Movements in which women crossed their hands in front of their chests were regarded as a way of demonstrating everything from elegant grace to coquettishness, depending upon the circumstances. The vent in a woman's yukata at that part of the sleeve where it joins the body of the robe then, has (or had) a twofold purpose. If a woman was in a social situation where modesty and a more formal decorum were required or expected, the vent served as a reminder. Every time she started to raise her arms or reached away from her body with them, she would be reminded by the puff of air coming through the vent that she was on the verge of taking a posture or making a movement that might not be entirely proper. No drafts at the vent and she was sure to be comporting herself in the way expected of a lady at that time. On the other hand, if she wished to flirt or to make some kind of romantic overture with a companion, the yukata-clad woman had only to make a subtle gesture to flash her *kyoei,* as the anatomical region in question is called. (Written with different characters but pronounced the same way, kyoei refers to "vanity." It is a homonymic twist ripe for all sorts of clever puns.)

The wide sleeves of a woman's yukata—the other part of the garment the American manufacturer decided to redesign for reasons of convenience—perform a similar function. As with kimono sleeves, they created all sorts of opportunities for the wearer to reach across her chest to brush them back, the movement graceful and meant to look appealing to the opposite sex. Getting rid of them is not at all different from sewing a panel across a low cut blouse to cover up the cleavage. The whole point of a blouse being low-cut is to expose cleavage. And the point here is that the components of a woman's yukata are not the result of a haphazard fashion accident. They evolved for a purpose. They have a significance, even though it may no longer be obvious. The point, too, is that in "redesigning" the yukata they were selling, the company who sent me their catalog had in reality butchered the robe. They did not re-create a more functional yukata, nor did they improve it—except by their own questionable standards. They produced an entirely different garment. Perhaps it had a superficial "Japanese" look; however, it had been robbed of its original style and function. It may have continued to work as a bathrobe or as loungewear—but should it be called a yukata? Arguably, no, because it is not. The unique characteristics of the true yukata have been stripped away. And here is what is more tragic: The individuals responsible for slicing off and sewing up the yukata's original design did so without ever knowing what they were doing, albeit with, I've no doubt, the best of intentions.

Does any of this sound vaguely familiar? Does it sound at all like all those who have been busy at work "redesigning" the various Japanese martial arts and Ways? Eager to set out to "improve" the arts? Or make the kata more entertaining, less repetitive, more relevant to today's conditions? Does it sound like those who restructure their karate to make it more realistic? I heard recently about a school that advertised jujutsu-like methods of grappling. They did not teach any methods by which to learn how to break one's falls safely because, as their advertisement explained it, "We're more interested in teaching you how to make *other* people fall down." Another school proudly noted they do not fool around with the pretentious folderol of etiquette, bowing and such. "People are too busy to spend time learning that sort of thing. They come for a workout or to learn to fight. If you want etiquette, read Emily Post."

It is almost too easy to ridicule these approaches. We need to remember, though, that the authors of such innovative attitudes do not hate the budo. Most of them who want to redesign it to meet whatever needs or desires they have probably care a great deal about these arts. Their intentions are not destructive. They are sincere and honest. They truly believe they are making changes for the better. (Sometimes I think they are genuinely puzzled at just how lazy or dull the great martial arts masters of earlier generations must have been. "Kata? Everybody knows the only way to learn self-defense is to do a lot of free-sparring." It is almost as if these types believe earlier generations in the dojo were stumbling along in the dark, just waiting for us today to come in and turn on the lights.) They take it for granted that their contributions are all for the best. They are essentially like the folks who redesigned the yukata. Those people really liked it, too. They just thought the changes they were inspired to make would improve things.

There are those who would suggest my analogy is, well, strained. They have a point. They could also suggest that many items in our everyday world have been altered and modified, and that rather than bastardizing them, it is really more an example of the evolution of things. The split-backed, swallowtail coats once worn by men had a function: they made riding a horse while wearing such a coat easier. While it can still be found in very formal wear like morning coats, modern suit coats for men no longer have that deep split; it lost its function and went out of style. Nobody's crying too much over this. If you are, you may still purchase or rent a swallowtail morning coat and knot up your silk Macclesfield tie and you're off to Ascot, suitably attired. So what's the big deal? The yukata itself evolved out of earlier clothing worn in Japan. Some Japanese began modifying more formal silk robes and gradually produced the yukata, and while there may have been some Muromachi-era curmudgeon version of me who was whining and moaning about those whippersnapper innovators throwing out the designs of those perfectly good Heian Period robes, the changes were wrought, and civilization in Japan did not grind to a halt as a result. So again, what's the big deal?

The deal, while it may not be big, is essentially this: We risk losing more than we think when we initiate changes in things we do not entirely or even adequately understand. I think it was the late environmental activist Edward Abbey who said that "the first law of tinkering is to save all the parts." When preparing a new and complex recipe for dinner tonight, you do not proceed with the task by casually substituting cayenne pepper for paprika. ("Hey, they're both dark red.") You do not consign to the blender ingredients the recipe indicates should be chopped. You don't leave out the salt since, what the heck, you can't even see it anyway, and so how important can it be?

The same is true of the environment, Abbey suggested. He was speaking of those who, for instance, drain "useless" swamps so parking lots might be built on the land, only to discover later that the swamp played a crucial role in filtering and purifying the aquifer that provides water for a city some miles away. The same logic applies to a yukata. And it applies to the budo. Oh, I know. Those who endeavor to create a new and improved martial Way are apt to talk a good deal about the vast experience they have brought to the table that makes their modifications seem calculated and worthy. As they do, take a look at them. Few are even into their forties. Almost none will have had more than a decade or two of actual training (and far less than that if we define training properly, i.e., under a legitimate teacher). The fact is, those who fool around with making changes in the combative arts they study almost inevitably do so without a knowledge of them that could be described as anywhere near comprehensive. Their understanding, even when it may be technically correct at some level, is usually fragmented. They have studied a grappling art for a while, then did a stint in the boxing ring. A couple of years of karate and an aikido seminar or two. The product? A thin broth, floating with odd, poorly matched chunks of this and that, some cooked, some not, poorly seasoned if at all—and they hope to pass it off as a nourishing stew. *Bon appétit.* The truth is that those who fool around with the budo are almost always engaging in such mischief without a knowledge of them that could in any way be described as sound or comprehensive. They are tossing out ingredients, adding others for the sake of convenience or personal preference. And whether they know it or not, they are in for some surprises the first time they sample a spoonful.

Those of us who *do* know what those vents in a woman's yukata are for, and who have seen them put to memorable use, do not object, it needs to be added here, if someone wants to use the yukata as an inspiration for creating an entirely new garment. I know of two very successful commercial enterprises who have bought old and worn kimono, taken them to pieces, then reassembled the fabric into dresses, vests, all kinds of clothing. The patterns are still visible, even though the kimono has been completely transformed. (One of my sensei has found a new use for old yukata. He has the material cut to make a lining for his *uwagi*, his cotton training jackets. In summer, the soft cotton of the recycled yukata absorbs moisture. In winter, it adds a welcome layer that makes the jacket warmer.)

Similarly, the field is wide open for those wishing to design a new combative art. Advances have been made in many related areas: exercise physiology; our understanding of how the body and mind interrelate in stressful situations like combat; techniques for improving coordination; the psychology of entering and dominating conflict. The careful and well-prepared innovator could come up with a fighting system, even one sufficiently sophisticated to be called an art. Yet in both cases, as it is with the "updated" yukata in the catalog and in the unique and new combat art, those presenting them need to be honest. Don't call what you're selling a yukata if it is not. That is not fair to the merchant who has gone to the trouble to procure or produce his own, historically authentic yukata. Nor is it fair to the customer who is looking for the real thing and who is not interested in your version. Do not call what you are doing "American karate" or "street jujutsu" or any other of those names that do little except unethically associate your stuff in the minds of potential students with karate or jujutsu or other arts with an historical provenance. Do not attempt to use the established names of these arts because you are not, in effect, transplanting them into a new environment. What you are doing is cobbling together something that is new. Advertise it as such. Let it stand or fall on its own worth, not propped up or dragged down by the borrowed name of something else.

So there it is. The connection between bathrobes and budo. Both of them can be redesigned, for good reasons or bad ones. The intention to redesign them can be completely sincere, or compromised by a desire for profit, or just an uninformed impulse to do something different. Yet having seen them in their original form, both yukata and budo, with all their beauty and uniqueness and value, I have trouble imagining why someone would bother to make changes. And I wonder why anyone would settle for less than the real thing.

6

Iai

Unsheathing the Sword

There is something electrifying about a swordsman, moving from a crouch or a kneeling position, or standing or walking, unsheathing a sword, cutting through the air with an audible *whoosh,* pausing, then returning the weapon, slowly, carefully, to the scabbard. In its modern form of iaido, or in one of the many classical versions still practiced by some ryu and which go by *iaijutsu* or various other names, the action has an undeniable drama. The practitioner moves with a calm grace. His breathing and his weapon are perfectly coordinated. His bearing is poised without theatrics, his timing measured with neither slack nor haste.

The opponent or opponents are imaginary. *Iai* is among the few traditional martial disciplines of Japan that is practiced without a live partner, for obvious reasons. The lack, somehow, does little to distract from the art. Practiced by its experts, imaginary enemies almost seem to take form. They attack and are repulsed, countered, overcome in a variety of ways. The swordsman dodges to the side, avoiding a blow, then leaps back in with a thrust. An overhead strike is parried, flicked away with the quickly drawn blade, then the attacker's wrists are slashed in an instant riposte. There are kata designed to simulate all manner of attacks, offensive and defensive. In nearly all its forms, ancient and modern, the action begins with a moment of tranquility. The swordsman, kneeling or standing, seems almost to be in a meditative state. The action arises out of a nearly complete stillness. It is cut, counter, cut, the sword flashing, the swordsman a swirl of motion. Then quiet. With a crisp snap, the blade is ritually cleaned of blood, then returned to the scabbard, always with a sense of quiet resolution. The quick slamming of the blade home and the loud bang as it goes back against the mouth of the scabbard is purely movie dramatics. In real iai, the finish is always a recapitulation of the start. Calm. Centered. Poised.

In the West most people who have seen or practiced iai have done so in iaido, the modern version of the art. Practitioners of iaido typically follow a series of *seitei-gata*—"standardized kata"—that have been synthesized, largely since the end of the last world war, from various classical sources. Much the way the King James version of the Bible was translated, by a group of experts who argued and compromised and worked toward a consensus, swordsmen in early modern Japan convened and came up with a set of kata for iaido. The ones they formulated were simplified or modified versions of the iai taken from different classical schools of swordsmanship. Other people of course, have gotten something of an education in iai by watching *chanbara*, the sword-slinging period dramas of Japanese movies and television, that are to feudal history what Westerns are to the historical realities of America's mid-nineteenth century. The lesson of this cinematic style of swordsmanship is mostly that wonders can be worked when the sword being drawn is not steel but a length of shaved bamboo covered with chrome, and that opponents can be felled like weeds before a scythe blade when the script calls for it.

Given the dramatic, almost romantic nature of iai, it is not surprising that many in the West have an interest in learning it. Nor is it surprising that a veritable host of "masters" of iai and other such instructors would have appeared on the scene. Most are staggeringly inept. Real teachers of iaido have no problem presenting credentials that are traced directly back to governing bodies in Japan. Those who are authentically licensed to teach the feudal-age varieties of iaijutsu that are a part of the curriculum of classical martial ryu are also well documented. Does the fellow proposing to teach you have a fantastic story of having been taught by a mysterious Japanese master who was, for some reason, living in Muncie, Indiana, and then vanished after imparting his skills? Uh-huh. In both classical and modern forms of iai, time, lots and lots of time spent under the direct supervision of an expert teacher, is necessary before receiving even the most basic permission to teach. Does the guy professing to be a "sixth-degree master-teacher" look too young to have attended the Senior Prom? Chances are his instruction came from watching Toshiro Mifune movies. Does he have, despite a lack of certification or any demonstrable connection to legitimate sources in Japan, a loyal, enthusiastic following? Numbers, along with a near-fanatical devotion to the teacher, are unfortunately not a reliable indicator of worth. In many cases, the more outlandish the claims of the instructor, the more determined his disciples are to believe them. It does little good to point out to these individuals the illogic, the oft-times obvious falsification of their studies; no one is more certain of his subject than he who is most ignorant of it. Those truly interested in the authentic arts of iai would be better off leaving these shallow souls, "masters" and acolytes alike, to their amusements, confident in the knowledge they will sooner or later abandon them in favor of some equally uninformed approach to the next popular diversion that comes along. The serious student (along with those who wish to be) should instead concern themselves with matters that will broaden and enrich their understanding of iai, even if circumstances deny them the opportunity to actually engage in its practice at the moment.

Certainly one of those subjects would be that of the name of the art itself. It seems simple. *Iai* is the word in Japanese that describes rapidly unsheathing a sword to use it for combat, either as a part of the draw or immediately thereafter. To really understand what iai means, however, is to delve into one of the most complex and subtle concepts of the Japanese martial arts. However, before we get any further down this road, a caveat. Imagine for a moment you are not a Westerner reading a book written by another Westerner, about a relatively obscure aspect of Japanese culture. Instead, you are a Japanese, reading a book about American culture, written by another Japanese. He is writing an essay on the phrase "good-bye." Yes, it seems like a simple way to bid farewell, the author tells you. Ah, but let's dissect the word, examine its etymology, he suggests. We see that it is a contraction from the original "God be with you." And what may we infer from this uniquely Occidental way of saying farewell to another? We see that their God is constantly on the minds and lips of these people, and that they invoke His blessings whenever they part. And so on and so on. Can you imagine how ridiculous such an explanation would be?

We can make a similar error into over-explicating a Japanese word like iai. If we do, I am a pretentious pedant. You are, at best, naive. So let us not travel along that path. Let us acknowledge that an examination of some terms—the *kara* of karate, the *ju* in judo come to mind—reveals nuance and some insight otherwise inaccessible. As it is with so many of the ideas inherent in the budo, if we take a moment to look at the word iai, consider its implications and the notion it represents, we are usually the better for it.

To begin, we have to know that not all martial ryu that include (or included, if they are no longer viable) combative sword-drawing in their curricula favor using the word iai as a description of the techniques or art they teach. *Batto* is another term. *Nuki-uchi, tsume-ai, rito, saya-no-uchi*; all of these and more appear in various ryu documents. The idea of modern iaido itself—as a synthesis of a number of classical kata organized not according to their respective ryu or for their distinctive characteristics, but rather as a generic approach to sword-drawing—arguably has its genesis in the study of Nakayama Hakudo (1869–1958). Nakayama was trained in several schools of swordsmanship, including some that specialized in iai, like the Omori ryu and the Muso Jikiden Eishin ryu. He eventually became the sixteenth headmaster of one branch of the Jinsuke-Eishin lineage of the art. Nakayama established his own system in the early 1930s, a composite of many of the styles of iai he had learned and which he called the Muso Shinden ryu.

After WWII, officials of the All Japan Kendo Federation, worried about the lack of swordsmanship among their ranks, used the template of the Muso Shinden ryu as a way of fashioning a standardized curriculum for teaching iai. Why would practitioners of kendo, the "Way of the Sword," fret about a decline in swordsmanship? Good question. The mechanics and dynamics of using a bamboo *shinai* for sportive purposes are dramatically different from the actual applications of wielding a steel sword. For cultural and practical reasons, kendo had by the middle of the twentieth century drifted so far in intent and method from battlefield swordwork as to be an art almost entirely divorced from its predecessor. Kendo's leaders, then and now, have been reluctant to admit this. They prefer to consider their Way as a seamless continuation of the sword art of the samurai. Instruction in drawing and cutting with a real sword within the ranks of modern kendo could be interpreted, depending upon your perspective, as a means of promoting this fiction or as an exercise in reminding *kendoka* of their roots.

The obvious approach to reinvigorating kendo would have been to invite senior exponents of the surviving classical ryu of swordsmanship to come and teach their individual arts in kendo dojo. Fat chance. Encouraging different ryu to teach and demonstrate would have meant dealing with rivalries between these traditions, some of which were generations old. It would also have caused friction had one system been promoted above others. (It would, as well, have brought swordsmen into kendo dojo who would have, deliberately or not, demonstrated the large gaps in modern kendo techniques as compared to older *gori-teki*, or "battlefield-efficient" skills.) So the officials of the Kendo Federation assembled several experts and together, in the late 1950s, they began hashing out a seitei-gata, or standardized set of kata. They came up with seven of them. In 1977, three more were added. Just before the turn of the twenty-first century, two more came into the mix, bringing the number of setei-gata to an even dozen.

While the number and actual performance of the seitei-gata have mutated, the name for the art was first suggested by Nakayama and has not changed since he did so. It was known as iaido as far back as 1932. Jukichi Yamatsuta, one of those selected to establish the standards for iaido, explained it this way: "Iai was an obvious choice. No other word commonly used to describe the exercises of drawing and cutting with the sword could so completely have expressed the nature of spirit and the body interacting as one."

The word Yamatsuta insisted so admirably represented the heart of his budo is perhaps best understood if we break it down into the two characters used in writing it. The first part of the word is written with a kanji pronounced as *i*. (It's a long "e" sound. It is amazing how many non-Japanese speakers routinely mispronounce iaido, reversing the syllables so it comes out "ai-i-da," which inevitably brings to mind a katana-brandishing opera tenor.) This kanji can also be pronounced as *iru* or *kyo*. I is the *kun* or native Japanese pronunciation. Kyo is the original Chinese, or *on* reading. (As a youngster learning some basic kanji during the sexually permissive sixties, I remember this character well, since it occurs in the phrase *dokyo suru*: "living together." Every magazine from Japan at that time seemed to carry an article about the shocking proliferation of dokyo suru over conventional marriage.)

The character of *i* means "to reside" or "to be in" a place. It carries the connotation of belonging and feeling comfortable in that space. In a more comprehensive light, *i* connotes an adaptability to or compatibility with one's surroundings. *Igokochi ga ii*—a phrase beginning with the *i* we're talking about here—means "to feel comfortably at home." All of us know people who have that quality of being able to fit in, to adjust to whatever variables they might encounter. They are the kind who seem to have little problem acclimatizing themselves to new places and new situations. It is as if their personalities are so geared they never feel a need to alter their behavior or demeanor to fit into a new or different environment. They can adapt to meet it while still being themselves.

The vagaries of fashion, peer pressure, and social influences don't seem to sway them or intimidate them. These are people who have a presence that suggests the quality of *i*. Similarly, we know people who appear to have a complete lack of that quality. They either shrink compulsively from unfamiliar situations or make frantic efforts to change and conform to their circumstances, even if only superficially.

All of us would like to believe we have some feeling for this quality. If we do not, we probably seek to find or to develop it. It is an admirable trait. However, there is something lacking in completeness in *i* by itself. Think of the well-known characters, historical and fictional, who have *i*. Alexander Selkirk, the marooned sailor who became the Robinson Crusoe of Daniel Defoe's famous novel, confronted almost unimaginable loneliness and deprivation, but he adapted to a solitary life on a Pacific island.

In Japanese history, the story of Sugawara Michizane is a good, real-life example of someone with *i*. Sugawara (845–903) was a scholar and poet during the Heian era, minister in the court of the Emperor Daigo. Rivals in the powerful Fujiwara clan plotted to cast Sugawara as treasonous in the eyes of the emperor; the scheme worked, and Sugawara was banished to the southern island of Kyushu. He accepted the punishment, and for the final two years of his life he continued to write poetry in exile. In accounts of both the fictional Robinson Crusoe and Sugawara, we see again and again that while they managed and adapted to privation, each lamented their separation from other people. Simply put, even though they conformed to meet the circumstances life had handed them, both wished for the chance to be with others and to be a part of society. No doubt they discovered during their solitude, if they did not already know it, that no matter how well one adapts to life's circumstances, there is still within the human soul a longing to interact with others. We are social creatures. To be able to exist alone is admirable. To enjoy a life without others, however, usually degenerates into little more than self-centeredness. This is where the second character in writing iai comes in: *ai.*

Unless they are students of the budo as well, Japanese language students might recognize *ai* by its alternate pronunciation, *go. Godo,* for instance, is a word commonly used among businesspeople at meetings in Japan. It means "a joint decision" or a "mutual agreement." In the dojo, *godo-geiko* is the word used to describe a training session where there is no teacher, just an informal gathering of members training together without anyone overseeing the instruction. *Ai,* or *awasu,* another way of pronouncing the character, is of course a very familiar term for martial artists. It is the one written for "aikido." It is also used in the term *ma-ai,* the distancing between opponents in combat. The original pictographic form of the character came from a drawing of a pot with a lid fitting over it. We might infer then, that *ai* implies a coming together of things that rightfully fit with one another. A correct relationship. Iai then, if we look at the word from a purely derivative point of view, means the ability of "residing" or "being present" within the context of relationships. It suggests adaptability in the midst of interaction. But hey—who are we interacting with in iaido? We've already noted that the art is a solo exercise. It is ironic that a word conveying relationships would be applied to an art that is among the very few Japanese combative disciplines almost exclusively performed alone.

There are at least two answers to that question. The first is that well, yes indeedy, that is what you get when you spend all your time breaking down words according to some ancient derivation and trying to read some kind of deep meaning into it: a dead end, since the origination of the word and what it came to mean hundreds of years later may be related only in the most tangential way. I don't like that answer for many reasons, not the least of which is that it doesn't give me much to write about. I also don't like it because it presumes our ancestors were careless or stupid in choosing words that expressed ideas. And so, this is the answer I prefer: To me, iai is about potential generated through initiative. If we have *i*, if we are "being present," then we have an awareness of who and where we are. We are not mentally asleep or drifting on autopilot. We are capable of meeting whatever circumstances may arise, or we have the power to create circumstances advantageous to us. If we can take these steps within the context of the society or people around us, we've got iai.

It *is* true that we are acting solo when we train in drawing and cutting with the sword. But we are not alone. Opponents attack in all sorts of ways, or we seize the initiative against them. If iaido or iaijutsu are to maintain their sense of reality, of combative efficacy, they have to paradoxically be "unreal" in that we cannot put others in danger by placing them in the path of a sharp sword in our training. So our practice of these arts becomes a practice of interaction with others who exist only in our minds. If we make a mistake, we risk only hurting ourselves. (That is not purely theoretical. Iai, when done with a blade, can be extremely dangerous. Practitioners have stabbed or cut themselves very seriously.) That also means we can challenge ourselves, and our potential is never limited; we are always dealing with an opponent who is just a little better, a trifle faster, against whom we must incessantly try to improve.

Iai, whether in the classical combative form of iaijutsu, or in the modern budo incarnation of iaido, is a terrifically demanding art. When we train against others, whether going through two-man kata or in contests, we can always find ways to overcome the person we are facing. Tricks, mental games, intimidation, or deceit; we can employ these as a way of making up for poor technique. In the solo art of iai, we cannot fall back on these. We have to learn to "be present," and to be completely honest with our enemy—one who knows every trick, every stratagem we might have at our disposal. He knows us well. He is the same one who faces us every time we look in a mirror. Challenging him becomes a medium through which we learn to deal with ourselves, in ways that make us better at interacting with others.

7

Gaman

Perseverence

"Hips" was the order of the evening. As in, "none of you are using them." The sensei at the aikido dojo where they let me train was unhappy with our application of hip muscles as we were moving forward. The problem is nearly universal in budo dojo. Karate-do, aikido, kendo; it doesn't matter. Most of us tend to be "top-heavy," in the sense that the majority of our sports and other physical activities are related to movements with the shoulders and upper body. In the Japanese budo, movement usually originates with muscles in the waist or hips. It's the hips that generate power in a karate punch, not the shoulders or arms. When the karateka kicks, he's driving not with his foot, but with the big muscles of his hips. In aikido, it may seem that the arms are doing the work in throws or pins. The real power, however, comes from the hips.

All kinds of supplemental training exercises are aimed at developing hip power in the dojo. On this particular evening, the sensei came into the dressing room and told us not to wear our *hakama* that night—just our jackets, pants, and belts. Once class began, he divided us into partners. One of the pair unwrapped his belt to loop it around the waist of the other. The "harnessed" *aikidoka* would begin stepping forward into left, then right front stances, making lunging punches with each step, each step being made against the resistance of his partner who was pulling steadily on the ends of the belt. It was a simple-enough exercise. The problem for me was twofold. One, my belt is frayed and tattered, the edges fuzzy, the black part only a thin gray strip down the middle, the edges a dirty white. Two, my partner Rick was built with dimensions similar to that of a sequoia tree. His frame is fleshed out like an anatomy chart. Chances were very good that he was going to snap my belt with his first step. He smiled at me and shook his head, unknotting his own belt so I could use it on him for the exercise. He didn't say anything about it, but he must have wondered why I didn't just get a new black belt; the thing I'm wearing is more like a rag than anything else. There is a certain élan in having one's uniform and belt sporting a worn, used look, to be sure. I've even heard of young black-belt wearers taking sandpaper to theirs to give them that frayed appearance of an old-timer. But there's a difference between "worn" and "worn-out." Mine was past the latter, and well into the embarrassingly shabby stage. Even so, I am not quite ready to retire it . . .

It was 1939. The system of awarding any kind of belts or *dan-i* ranks within martial arts schools was still relatively recent, an innovation that had begun with judo's founder, Jigoro Kano, back in the late nineteenth century. Ranking standards were still being codified by the All Japan Kendo Federation, a process that had begun a decade earlier. It was a different age. There were still swordsmen around, plenty of them, who had very practical talents with their weapons. Their perspective was still essentially feudal. In many kendo dojo, the action was much more like that on a battlefield than in mere sport, especially in terms of energy and fighting spirit. There was not much slacking off, and standards were high. So the fact that the Federation presented a *yondan*—or fourth-degree rank— to a kendoka only twenty-four years old meant not that he'd won a few matches in contests or that he was a sincere fellow who always showed up to class on time. It meant his skills were extraordinary.

Nobuyuki Sakai was an exceptional man. He had graduated from the old Meiji University and had been accepted to continue his work there toward earning a law degree. He was a prominent member of the university's kendo club. A marriage broker hired by his parents had arranged an engagement with a young woman from a good family, through *omiai* (matchmaker-arranged dates). It wasn't just Sakai for whom the proverbial livin' was easy. Japan was emerging as a major power in Asia, economically and militarily. The worst of the worldwide depression was past. Recovery in Japan and elsewhere was slow but steady. The spirit of the country was bright and optimistic (if blinkered by propaganda and contrived stories in newspapers about how thankful the rest of Asia was for having been invaded and enslaved). After centuries of isolation, the country embraced foreign culture, and there was an avid interest in international affairs and in getting to know the world outside the borders of the island nation. Thousands of young men took advantage of Japan's wealth and left to study or travel abroad. Sakai was among them. He took a year off before starting his graduate studies, to visit family friends who had immigrated to the Territory of Hawaii. A month after receiving his yondan, Sakai left Yokohama on a ship bound for Honolulu. With him went his kendo gear, armor and shinai, along with a new black belt, a gift from his teacher. (Kendo practitioners do not normally use the belts worn by judo or karate exponents. Sakai's belt was wider and longer than these, worn under the hakama to help keep the training jacket closed and to hold a sword in its scabbard when they practice using a live blade in kata.) His teacher had had some kanji embroidered in gold thread on the end of the belt. It read *gaman*: "perseverance."

Life in Hawaii was at its fabled best. The weather, the beaches, the relaxed lifestyle—it all appealed to Sakai. The Japanese presence in Hawaii was so pervasive there had been serious talk about annexing the islands as another prefecture of Japan, so even though his English was minimal, he had little trouble becoming acclimatized to life there. After he'd had his fill of sightseeing, Sakai took a job working on a sugar cane plantation. It paid as well as most field labor then, and more important to him, the job allowed him to spend the days in the sunshine, with the physical part of cutting and hauling cane keeping him in shape for the kendo training he did almost every evening. In addition to his job and his kendo, Sakai managed to find the time to fall in love, with a girl named Midori—which was a problem because Sakai was more or less legally contracted to a marriage back in Japan. To a woman who was, of course, not Midori.

"That kind of stuff has a way of sneaking up on you," he said, recalling it many years later. "I sweated and worried a long time. I was really in love with Midori. The family I was living with in Hawaii were on me like heck about it. They liked Midori fine. But they said I was going to make my parents ashamed and get them in a lot of hot water if I didn't go through with the marriage back in Japan."

When it was time for Sakai to return to Japan, he went to the local consulate and got his stay extended by six months. Part of it was because of Midori; part of it was because he enjoyed Hawaii so much, and working out in the fields had given him a taste for farming. Work in the cane fields was long and hard, but he was fast becoming accustomed to it. And he relished the camaraderie he found there, working with Chinese, Japanese, and Filipino immigrants, along with local Hawaiians. He justified his stay by telling himself that in exchange for another six months in Hawaii, he would write his parents and ask them to nullify the marriage agreement in Japan.

"The day I sat down to write the letter," he remembered, "I got one from them. They explained that the girl I was supposed to marry had changed her mind. She wanted out of the arrangement." It was, he said, "one of the happiest days of my life." Free to marry Midori, Sakai set about with plans to do just that. They would stay in Hawaii just until the following spring, when they would return as a couple so he could start school in Tokyo. They were wed in a Shinto ceremony in Kailua, in September of 1941.

The newlywed Sakais moved in with his bride's family. They had already booked passage on a ship to Japan when, on a Sunday in December, the planes with the big red suns on their wings came over the islands, on their way to Pearl Harbor. Within days, Sakai found himself in a detention center at Sand Island, near Honolulu, along with many other citizens of Japanese ancestry. Once the hysteria and fear calmed, and after many local business and plantation owners spoke up for them, most of those detained were released. There were no mass roundups as would soon be happening on the West Coast of the mainland. Sakai, however, was a different story. He was not a citizen of the territory of Hawaii. He held a Japanese passport. His new father-in-law also happened to be a staunch Japanese patriot. These types existed in Hawaii in those days. They may have been living away from Japan for decades, and may have become almost completely assimilated into life outside Japan. Yet inside, they still considered themselves Japanese in a fanatical, almost mystical sense. Sakai's father-in-law was a player in local Japanese organizations and spoke frequently and publicly about Japan's divine right to rule Asia.

"He had stacks of pro-Japanese newspapers and magazines in the house," Sakai recalled. And he was not hesitant about insisting Japan's attack on the U.S. fleet was justified. It was more than enough for the military authorities to order him and his family to be shipped to the mainland, where they would be processed and sent to one of the relocation camps.

"I had no choice," Sakai said. "My mother-in-law wasn't in good health. I couldn't have left my wife to take care of both her parents."

And so, when he should have been packing for the trip back to Japan and law school, planning a life there, he prepared to sail instead in the opposite direction, as a prisoner of the U.S. Army, headed for a place he'd never heard of. Like the others, he and Midori were allowed to take few possessions other than their clothes. He did not have any room for his kendo gear. The only thing he took was the black belt that had been given to him by his teacher in Japan.

The contrast must have been shocking. From a neat frame house close to an Oahu beach, Sakai and his wife set up housekeeping in a dormitory with thin, uninsulated walls and a leaky, tar-paper roof. It was like an oven in the hot summer sun of Arkansas in July. In the winter, it was chilly and drafty. Privacy was impossible. The Sakai family, like everyone else behind the wire, ate in a communal mess hall, showered in big community facilities; even their bedtime was determined by a lights-out policy. Along with the constant regulation of every aspect of their lives, the pressures inherent in living so closely with others, and the extremes of climate, Sakai had even bigger problems.

"My English was mostly limited to 'hello', 'heck no', stuff like that," he said, along with a variety of colorful but comparatively useless swearwords he had picked up in the cane fields. He had no way of communicating with the authorities at the camp to find out what was happening to his family back in Japan, or to let them know where he was.

"For all they knew, I'd disappeared off the earth," he said.

Although some in the camp assured Sakai their internment couldn't last long, he also had no idea if he would still be allowed to enroll in the university after such a long absence, or whether he would even be a citizen of Japan once the war was over. Partly to distract himself from his fears and frustrations, and partly because of his interest in growing things, Sakai started to work in the gardens being planted by the internees.

"I spent a lot of time talking to the older guys," Sakai said. "They knew *everything* about the soil—how to fertilize, how to space the plants. I learned a lot."

Sakai also kept up his kendo practice as well as he could. He found a piece of pipe about the length of a kendo shinai, although being made of metal, it was much heavier. He used it to practice *suburi*, the basic striking exercises of the art, moving back and forth to keep his legs strong and flexible. He met other *issei* and *nisei* who had trained in kendo. Using makeshift equipment— "We made chest protectors out of pieces of cardboard inside canvas"—they formed classes. The dusty, uneven wooden floor of the camp's recreation hall was a world away from the polished dojo floor at Meiji University where Sakai might have been. But in a homemade hakama and uwagi and wearing his belt, Sakai took up his equally homemade shinai without any complaint. "*Shigata ga nai*," he told his wife. "It cannot be helped."

The residents of the camp who assured Sakai their intern-ment would be short were, of course, wrong. The camps were open for the duration of the war and beyond, while the U.S. government struggled to decide how to get so many people back out into the country. While the country was still at war, several of the men inside volunteered to go into the army. Sakai, being a Japanese citizen, did not have this as an option. Instead, he spent his time behind the barbed wire of the Arkansas camp tending to the gardens and practicing his kendo. A few months after the Japanese surrender that marked the end of the war, the Sakais were freed.

"Hard to tell you what that was like. Like waking up from a long bad dream. We couldn't even believe it was happening for a while," he said. "But we really woke up when we realized we had to support ourselves; make a living, start thinking about some kind of future outside the camp."

His plan of becoming a lawyer was clearly out of the question. Sakai was already in his early thirties, well past the age for embarking on such an education. He had no money and no idea if Meiji University was still standing, for that mat-ter. Even so, he reasoned, educated men his age might well be at a premium in postwar Japan. Surely he could make a decent living there. Efforts at contacting his family had failed, but communication between the United States and Japan was still shaky. And even if the worst had happened and his parents had not survived the war, Sakai, as their only son, would have inherited their house and property. If they were still alive, they would need his help. Going back to Japan, then, was the plan. To raise the money, Sakai found a job working on a farm in Oklahoma. His wife got a job nearby in a chicken farm. Both often put in days that began at sunup and lasted until it was dark. They lived in a small house—"a shack, really," he remembered—on his boss's farm. Even then, Sakai continued his kendo training.

"In the evenings I used to go out and swing a heavy shinai in a pasture," Sakai recalled. "The feel of that long grass on my bare feet, cool when the dew started coming onto it; so nice."

Within two years, Sakai and his wife had put aside enough money to get to Japan. Then he heard, finally, from his relatives there. "There were only a couple of cousins still alive by then," he explained. "When I finally got in touch with them, they had some bad news." In one of the first bombing raids carried out against Japan by the United States, both Sakai's parents had been killed. The family home was rubble. With Sakai missing, an uncle had inherited the property on which the house stood; but he'd lost it in one of the many half-baked financial schemes that plagued postwar Japan. It was Sakai's wife Midori who convinced him there was nothing to return to in Japan. Instead, they accepted an offer made by Sakai's boss to buy a piece of his land.

On their own farm, the couple worked just as hard. Sakai made a friend of the county farming agent and volunteered his land for testing some of the new methods of farming, like contour tilling and crop rotation. He experimented on his own with several crops. He settled on soybeans. The Sakais were a part of the growing affluence of postwar America. By the early sixties, they had more than tripled their land holdings. "And we had a new Ford station wagon," he said. They had enough work on their farm to require extra workers. Some of those they hired, in fact, were the sons of friends with whom Sakai had practiced kendo in the internment camps. The opportunity to work on the Sakai farm meant college tuition for several of these workers; they became the first generation of native-born Japanese-American professionals. In a certain kind of irony, the Sakai farm became one of the first farms in the Midwest to make a contract with buyers in Japan, who were increasingly purchasing American soybeans to make everything from tofu to soy sauce there. Sakai also built a small kendo dojo on his farm. In the sixties, it was one of the few places in the midwestern part of the United States where kendo training was regularly conducted.

"We had about fifteen guys training, four nights a week," he said. "In the summer, we'd have all the windows open and you could hear the *kiai* for about half a mile away. We'd have some of those old Oklahoma farmers come by and stand in the doorway and watch." He laughed. "They thought we were crazy."

Despite the obstacles he overcame, the disappointments he suffered, Sakai never considered himself an extraordinary character. He never expressed any feelings of having been cheated or deprived of what should have or could have been his. He was a devout Presbyterian; he'd converted when he married Midori in Hawaii. Even so, he maintained a stubborn, almost instinctive belief in the Buddhist notion that we are all bound to a certain, immutable course in our lives, and we have little choice but to adapt and endure. Whatever happens in life, as he'd told his wife back in the camps, "It can't be helped." When he had left Japan back in the thirties to go to exotic Hawaii, he was the first person in his family who had ever left that country. Did he have any trepidation about it?

"No," he shrugged. "You gotta figure, whatever's gonna happen is gonna happen." He faced the trip with a steadfastness of spirit. It was the same steadiness with which he later accepted the loss of a carefully planned career. He lost a family, lost his freedom for four years, lost a sizable inheritance in Japan. And always, it was shigata ga nai. It can't be helped.

In 1972, Sakai took his wife on a trip back to his homeland. Although he was in his eighties, he brought along his kendo gear. He was still training. His reputation in kendo circles had grown. In Japan he was going to be awarded, more than thirty years after he'd made the fourth *dan*, a promotion to *godan*, the fifth level of black belt. So he did not take along the frayed belt, the one with the character for "perseverance" sewn into its end. It was time, he said, for a new one. He gave the old one to a friend.

As I said, my belt's in bad shape. The place where it is knotted is fuzzy and stringy and it's a little too long for me; always has been. But I think I will keep it for a while longer. At least until the last of the gold threads on one end are gone.

8

Sensei

If you feel that the teacher is a real teacher, then toss
away your ideas and learn.
>   —Hozoin Kakuzenbo In-ei

Some debts ya never can repay.
>   —Doc to Suzy in John Steinbeck's *Cannery Row*

It was in Edo, the old capital city, in the summer of the second
year of Ansei (1856), when the rumors began. At first, Ishi, the
senior student of the late headmaster, ignored them. He had
heard tales that were being repeated throughout the neighborhood, of ghostly apparitions flitting around the vicinity of the
master's grave. Japan has always been a superstitious place.
Ghost stories—tales of haunted cemeteries and temples and any
place at all isolated—were the stuff of legend and literature.
And of the feudal Japanese version of our own urban lore, stories told again and again by those who had a friend whose

brother knew a guy who *definitely* was there when it happened, when the ghost came right up from behind a wall of grave markers, wailing, spectral eyes bulging. Furthermore, hot summer is prime time for ghosts in Japan, like Halloween is for ours. (There's some suggestion that ghosts, or more accurately, ghost stories—are popular in summer in Japan because the chills they can give are a pleasantly scary way to cool off.)

In the case of Ishi's master, the ghost was not making regular appearances. It was only on those nights in the warmer months, when big thunderstorms rolled in off the ocean. Lightning flickering, thunder a far-off rumble, and the first patter of big, fat raindrops; that was when those passing by the cemetery insisted they were seeing a shadowy figure lurking around the grave of Yamaoka Seizan, the martial artist who had founded the Yamaoka ryu of *sojutsu*, the art of the spear.

The stories had become so common, Ishi finally decided to investigate. A few evenings later, just after the neighborhood warden had come by, clacking his wooden clappers together to remind everyone to be careful of their fires, came the first signs of a storm. A line of purplish clouds appeared on the horizon, coming closer and closer and looming, finally, up over Edo Bay. Ishi stepped into his clogs and set out for the cemetery. He found a place along one wall of the cemetery where he could see Yamaoka's grave and still huddle out of the rain that was sure to come. Twenty minutes passed; the air got thick and damp. The first gusts of the storm's wind kicked up dust around him. Ishi smiled to himself. His teacher would not have liked this weather, not at all. Yamaoka was a fiend in the dojo, fearless— but he was terrified of thunderstorms. Yamaoka had always dreaded the start of the rainy season, a fact he believed he kept successfully to himself, unaware that as it is with all a teacher's foibles, his students knew it well.

It had become almost completely dark by now. And the wind was making so much noise it was hard to isolate any sound. That's why Ishi had no idea from whence the apparition came. Suddenly it was there, looming up beside Yamaoka's grave. The hair on the back of Ishi's neck was standing up, his scalp tingling with fright. Then came a flash of lightning and he could see the "ghost." It was Ono Tetsutaro, another senior student of Yamaoka's. As Ishi watched from his hiding spot, he saw Ono kneel down to sit beside Yamaoka's grave. Then he heard Ono. "Don't be afraid, sensei," Ono said. "Ono Tetsutaro is here, and I will not leave until the storm is past."

In most practical terms, the title of *sensei* is translated as "teacher." It can also carry the connotation in Japanese of "mentor." It can, as well, be used to describe a physician, a school teacher or professor, or anyone who has some respected skills. Sensei can also be used in a jocular sense. A guy who is balancing more than one girlfriend, for instance, can be nicknamed "Sensei," as a tribute to his adroitness in finessing the opposite sex. Most Japanese, in using the word, have some understanding of what it means in these contexts. In other words, if a Japanese tells another Japanese in my presence that I am a sensei, I usually do not object. They are merely explaining that I am responsible for teaching or leading others in budo training. That's all. They are not implying I am a Great & Peerless Master. Unfortunately, perhaps because it is a borrowed word, when sensei is used as a title in English, there is considerable confusion about its meaning. For some, sensei means one is at some fabulous level of expertise. For others, it is a title for anyone who teaches a class. So if the dojo teacher is out of town on business and has left in charge some brown-belt kid to lead the beginner's class, he is called "sensei" by those in the class. Some budoka adopt a policy of never referring to anyone who is not directly their instructor as a sensei. While this can sometimes be socially awkward, it has much merit. (It should go without saying that a person who refers to himself as a sensei, or who demands or expects to be called that—even if you are not under his tutelage—is not really worthy of any serious consideration as a teacher of any kind.)

Following the example of many of my seniors, I make it a habit to correct those non-Japanese who address me as "sensei." I do so not because I have two standards, but because in the latter case, as I said, there are a number of varying connotations when the word is not used in a Japanese context, and some of them are misleading in the extreme. To illustrate my point: After giving a public demonstration of budo, I was approached by a spectator with a question. "Sensei," he said to me as he came up. Reflexively, I responded that I am not a sensei. He blanched slightly, then ventured "*Shihan?*" The word, used almost entirely in written form or in very formal circumstances, is something like "Master." In other words, he was concerned he had offended me by referring to me as a mere and lowly sensei when I was "obviously" on a much loftier plane. Such preposterous conclusions demonstrate the confusion we have with the title of sensei. Maybe it would clarify matters somewhat if we were to look at who the sensei is. Admittedly, this is my own perspective; it is the way I qualify someone for the title, and others' opinions may differ. It should, though, give some guidance in understanding the notion of the sensei.

In any art or discipline, the teacher is of necessity a central figure. In most cultures, those who teach are regarded with some respect. In the modern martial Ways—judo, karate-do, aikido, and so on—this regard often goes far beyond respect and reaches an embarrassing stage of outright adulation in some cases. The sensei is sometimes regarded as would be the leader of a cult or a religious movement. He is elevated in the estimation of his followers into a sage, a master who lives in an entirely different realm than the rest of us. If they have never been exposed to it before, anyone who has seen the behavior of these students in the presence of their leader will be surprised. His disciples will rush to carry any of the sensei's bags, to fold his hakama after training if that garment is worn as part of the art's uniform (as in aikido), to attend to his every need. The modern budoka should know that this emphasis may be common in his particular art, but it is not nearly so heavily pronounced in the classical koryu.

The teacher in these martial arts that remain from the feudal period maintains a status of authority and respect usually not because of his personality or even his expertise, but more because he represents a direct conduit to the real focus of the trainee's veneration and loyalty—which is the ryu itself. As a member of say, the Kifurushi ryu, your teacher is the link between you and the founder of the ryu. While his energy and personality will influence training in the dojo, they are, if the transmission has been proper, a reflection of the energy and personality of the ryu. His importance in the dojo is directly related to his role as a link to the tradition of the ryu. This distinction may be subtle, but it is crucial to comprehending how the image of the sensei has developed.

The tale of Ono Tetsutaro's visit to the cemetery to comfort the spirit of his dead teacher occurred, significantly, in the middle decades of the nineteenth century, almost 250 years after major warfare had ceased in Japan. Many combative ryu were in a period of transition. The ryu derived its reputation not from the success of its members on the battlefield any longer, but from their records in individual duels and in their ability to attract numbers. In this context, the charisma and prowess of the teacher began to play a far bigger role. It is a role that would become even more important as so many of the martial arts in early modern Japan shifted their goals to sport or athleticism, and to the advancement of social, cultural, and moral values.

In the modern budo, the equation between the teacher and the system being taught is almost completely flipped from the feudal, koryu model. A famous teacher attracts students who are less likely to feel any loyalty to the art than they are to learning from a respected authority with a reputation. Scarcely a week passes when a plane landing in mainland Japan or on Okinawa does not disembark a budoka passenger who has traveled in some cases thousands of miles just to train with a sensei. Thousands of martial artists throughout the world have passed up opportunities for advancements in their schooling or in their careers for the chance to study with these teachers. Such enthusiasm borders on veneration. There is a temptation to scoff at this. The adoration of the sensei seems like just another version of the uncritical fawning over celebrities or sports figures. In some cases, it may be. Unfortunately, in other cases, it can be worse. The sensei becomes a father figure. Or a "he's got all the answers for me" kind of guru. Emotionally needy students invest in their teachers a familial or spiritual attachment that is often a perfect setup for situations that can lead to rejection or abuse. If the mature, experienced sensei is aware of the feelings of his student, he may try to steer the student into a more realistic view of the relationship. If not—and with appalling frequency—the "if not" is more often the case, the sensei takes advantage of the student. It can come in the form of sadistic brutality as the teacher vents his anger or frustration on students; as sexual exploitation; financial leeching; or just as a form of emotional intimidation. Instead of making his students more independent and self-confident, the teacher manipulates them in such a way as to guarantee a continual need for his approval.

While there are numerous instances of this kind of despicable behavior, a picture of the relationship between sensei and student based on these bleak examples is distorted. The connection between a teacher and his disciple is healthiest and most productive and least likely to be perverted when it is cemented with the glue that has always held best in these arrangements. Like most other relationships in Japanese culture in the past, and for the most part, in the present, interaction between a sensei and his students is bound with Confucian ethics.

The reader who may have been drifting off might be brought up short by this. Confucianism? Isn't that Chinese? Yes. But Confucian values and philosophy were imported to Japan as early as the fourteenth century, brought by Buddhist monks returning from their studies in China. Concurrent with the rise of military power in Japan from that time on, Confucian philosophy played an increasingly important role in Japanese life. Its pronounced insistence on a strict social order made it more than palatable for the authorities; it reinforced their positions and made the other classes less inclined to question their own lower status in the hierarchy. Children were to respect and obey their parents, a relationship that mirrored the respect and obedience due one's seniors in all aspects of life. Leadership was a part of the natural order, a convention of the stern yet benevolent "we know what's best for you" type of paternalism. (Of course, in the original versions of Chinese Confucianism, the power of leaders was to arise from their superior ethical sensibilities and not through military might. That wasn't a big hit in a Japan ruled by the bow and sword. The tension between these competing principles for establishing rule, the imported Confucian reliance on rule through scholarly accomplishment and ethical excellence, and the samurai's belief of power gained through caste-derived privilege and warrior muscle, was to characterize politics and social mores from the feudal period through today.)

The relationship between students and teachers was inevitably shaped in Japan by the strictures of Confucian thought. The status of the teacher was unchallenged for the student. From the teacher's perspective, he had an ethical obligation to educate those under his instruction. It worked, in other words, both ways. This critical aspect is often lost on teachers today who would be sensei in a traditional sense. They may be aware to some extent of the influences of Confucianism. They tend, though, to regard that as a system in which the student owes all to his mentor and must be willing to assume any hardship, withstand any abuse, in order to learn; and the teacher, in contrast, is expected only to dispense wisdom from his lofty perch. In reality, the bond between student and teacher is one of mutual effort. Both are expected to give. The student is dependent upon the teacher for his advancement; the teacher depends equally on the student to preserve and continue the skills he wishes to pass on. Without this critical bond, the role of the sensei is warped or perverted. He may teach or impart knowledge or skills, but he is not participating in the tradition of an educational system that will insure those skills and learning will continue on to future generations.

Aside from this understanding of the mutual duties and responsibilities of the teacher and his student, what other qualities does the sensei need? Well, naturally, he has to be technically proficient in his craft. He has to possess the ability to lead, not only within the circle of his students but within the organization or the ryu of which he is a member. Finally, he must be able to communicate the methods of his art to a wide range of students. Qualifications like these seem self-evident. When a potential student considers asking a teacher to be his sensei, however, he usually does so almost blindly. The teacher's school is near the student's home or work. A friend is training with the sensei and recommends him. The student can be distracted by the extraneous. He sees a dojo with its own sauna or Jacuzzi, or with rows of trophies. Often, too, a would-be student has preconceived notions as to what a sensei should be like, based upon stories, movies, or other fictional or romanticized accounts. When a sensei fails to live up to these standards, the student passes on the chance to train. If we look at the three criteria that have traditionally made a good sensei in the budo, we can avoid some of these errors in judgment. We can also have a clearer and more meaningful idea of what a sensei is.

Technical ability as a measure of the sensei doesn't seem too tough to figure. The sensei has to know what he is doing. Careful here, though. The measure of ability is not always so simple. American servicemen who practiced judo at the Kodokan in Tokyo after the Second World War were surprised to see an old man walking carefully out onto the main practice mats. They were told he was there to teach a class for some of the younger instructors. Without any ceremony, the instructors lined up and bowed and class began. One by one, they approached the old man. When they did, and took grips with him, he proceeded to throw them about as if they were complete beginners. By the end of an hour, the young teachers, all in fine physical shape, were a battered and thoroughly tired lot. The old man, who was judo's last tenth-dan, Kyuzo Mifune, appeared on the other hand to have taken about thirty years off his frame with the workout.

I saw Yoichiro Yoshikawa, the late headmaster of Kashima Shinto ryu, not too long before he died. In the dojo he was easily able to beat the timing of some of his best students, men who were almost half his age. In tests of strength, weight lifting, or the ability to deliver power, both Yoshikawa and Mifune would almost certainly have lost to younger exponents. The difference was in their more finely developed sense of rhythm and timing, their application of correct distancing. True, in a fighting art in which pure physical skill is dominant, as a person ages, his ability will decrease. In the budo, muscular strength is without a doubt important, but—especially when weapons are involved—other, more subtle factors must be considered.

At the other end of the spectrum, sadly, are those who profess to be sensei but who refuse to ever demonstrate their art because, "it's so deadly I'd kill my students if I went against them, even in practice." Given the appearance and condition of some of these, perhaps this lethality might best be implemented if they were to fall on top of one of their students.

The budo are not magic. They cannot imbue someone with superhuman powers that are immune to the effects of age. If you expect a sensei in his sixties or seventies to perform on the same level as a practitioner in his twenties, you are bound to be disappointed, especially if your expectations are based entirely on easily observable factors. Watch to see the timing, however, or the sense of judging exactly when and where to move. You may find that the sensei's technical skills in these areas more than compensate for any that may have been degraded by time.

The matter of taking responsibility within the system or the ryu is another distinguishing characteristic of the sensei. These obligations are not typically a matter of concern for the student. Still, it is informative to watch the way in which the sensei meets these. He is providing a lesson for the student in another Confucian principle, that of duty. Filial respect—the respect one has for those in positions above and below him—implies a commitment to duties owed. Indeed, one way of demonstrating respect

in the conventions of Confucian thought has always been to ful-
fill obligations. The individual is important primarily as he re-
lates to the whole, according to a fundamental precept of
Confucianism. The sensei understands he is descended from a
lineage, or that he is a component in an art. But he is not the art
unless—in those rare cases, which frankly raise eyebrows among
serious martial artists—it is one he has founded. And even then
he must acknowledge his own teachers.

Back in the sixties, I remember going along with some
aikido students to an airport in the Midwest. We were all going
to collect their sensei, who had been in Japan for several months.
The sensei was among the highest-ranked aikidoka in the country. In the Midwest, where the art was still uncommon, he was
the source of aikido instruction. His students assumed he must
have been a major figure in aikido back in Japan. He was coming home and bringing with him another teacher who was coming for a long visit. I will never forget the look of surprise on the
students' faces when their sensei came off the plane toting his
bags as well as those of the other sensei, who was senior to him.
"We never saw Sensei as subservient," one of them told me later,
still shaking his head. Their sensei, of course, was not subservient at all. He was merely behaving correctly, taking his
place in the scheme of seniority within the art. No matter how
long your teacher has been training, it is a good bet he has seniors. The way in which he behaves toward them is a very reliable
indicator as to what kind of teacher—and person—he is.

The ability to communicate effectively to others is another
standard by which the sensei should be judged. Not all of them
are great at it. It is clear, looking back through history, that some
of the most legendary and skilled figures in the history of martial art were failures as teachers. Miyamoto Musashi taught others the art of swordsmanship, an art at which he indisputably

excelled. But he left few students who matched or exceeded him. Reading about his life, one is left with the impression he spent much of it caring only about building his own reputation and ability; the rest of it, he spent feeling frustrated at his limitations in explaining his art or passing it on.

The problem of poor teachers is well known. Teaching skills can themselves be taught. Education majors must attend classes instructing them on how to present lessons and on ways to determine how well the material they present is being absorbed. However, the personality of the individual who wishes to teach does figure to some extent in the success they can achieve as a teacher. Some have what it takes; some do not. The first hurdle he must overcome is his own ego. A good teacher must have the heartfelt and sincere desire to see his students become better than he is. This is not easy. It requires no small measure of graciousness, humility, and self-sacrifice to be willing to lead students to where you are and then beyond. Some parents have difficulty doing that with their own children. There is a sober maturity required in undertaking such a task for students. It is rare that a teacher will come along who will deserve the comment Phillip Larkin is supposed to have made to Cyril Connolly when they met at Auden's funeral: "Sir, you formed me." The sensei must always bear in mind the tremendous responsibility he has for shaping character. Fundamental to that is the willingness to see his student go further than he himself has gone.

The teacher must also be broad-minded enough in his attitudes and in his repertoire of talent to teach those who may be different from him, in terms of everything from temperament to social background to physical type. He must have standards. The integrity of the art must be maintained. Yet he must also allow for individual differences in his students, and be able to develop these. Despite common criticisms that the traditional budo are restrictive, useful only for turning out cookie-cutter clones of the teacher, there is actually a wide range of what is "correct" in a technique or in the embodiment of the art. "Everyone's front kick must look exactly the same." No, everyone's front kick must usefully and correctly apply principles inherent in the style of karate being taught. "Kata is just a stultifying exercise in copying a teacher, with no room for individual creativity." Nope. Kata is a form that allows the adherent, through successive practice and advancement, to make a fundamental concept uniquely his own. This is the job for the sensei—a daunting one as he looks out onto a class that is widely disparate in nearly every way.

In visiting a modern budo dojo, watch the sensei. Does he teach only his "specialties?" Or a wide range of techniques over the course of several classes? If he is unusually short or tall, small or large, does he confine his teaching to strategies and methods useful only to those of a similar body type? Logically, anyone who is well trained in an art should be able to instruct another successfully if that other person is the same size and of the same personality and background. The sensei, however, has to deal with all manner of students. While he may seem to be paying no particular attention to any of them, he teaches in such a way that benefits all of them. Communication at this level is a necessity for the sensei. A whole wall of trophies and certificates cannot compensate for a lack of it.

This final qualification I set out for a sensei—the ability to communicate with a wide range of students—is one we should not leave too quickly and without some qualification. That a sensei should be able to relate his art to students of varying body types, backgrounds, and so on, is *not* to imply any and all must be accommodated in the dojo. Quite the contrary, and here's why: Some prospective students of the budo, like some of the population in general in our generation, have been raised to take very seriously the tenets of all kinds of manifestations of popular psychology. In books, on television programs, in schools, and perhaps in private sessions, they have been led to believe their emotional problems and neuroses are matters of near-global consequence. Often fussed over by well-meaning parents and school counselors, these people can develop quite distorted egos. (And in the budo, as in life, there is no real difference between an ego that is too large and one that is stunted.) When they find their way to a sensei, they can bring along with them a firm belief that the budo is a path toward solving all their problems, both real and imagined. And they believe just as strongly that while "other" students may progress under the normal course of instruction at the dojo, they have such extraordinary needs as to require and deserve exceptional attention.

These attitudes surface in all kinds of ways. The sensei must meet each of them and deal with them. Does he allow the male chauvinist, for example, to train only with other men because the fellow claims to feel discomfort at the possibility of injuring one of the "little ladies"? Does he set up special "women-only" classes for those of a feminist ideological bent? It is almost a certain bet the karate sensei will encounter a young student who will ask to be excused from participating in the kata training of the dojo since "he wants to be a tournament free-sparring champion," and kata is perceived by him as a waste of training time. Another student may wish to pass on the same unrehearsed sparring, explaining that such aggression is too frightening or painful to deal with. Students may object to bowing or other rituals, citing religious objections. If his own training has been inadequate, the teacher will succumb to the considerable pressure these types can exert. In doing so, he risks assuming the role of an unqualified therapist. Or that of a merchant, giving the customer what he wants. If he is a real sensei, however, he will be understanding and patient. But he will demonstrate to his students by his attitude and his actions that the first and most important lesson they must learn as budoka is that their "special needs" exist almost entirely in their own minds and nowhere else. And that they must train in their chosen budo more or less exactly as everyone else.

This will seem harsh, almost cruel at times. A student may have long cherished a desire to come to a particular sensei's dojo and to apprentice under him, absorbing the secrets of life as he follows the Way. And here is the sensei, the man or woman so much admired, telling him, in effect, to get over himself. It all sounds distressingly like the brutality of a thoughtless high school football coach telling one of his fullbacks to "shake it off" when the player is showing him an arm with the ends of splintered bone sticking out. Indeed, there are people who will come to the dojo whose psychological or emotional problems are real and severe. In these cases, while it would be nice to believe the budo can work miracles, it is best if such people are directed at getting the professional help they need.

The budo can probably help a mentally healthy practitioner stay that way. It is snake oil to advertise them as a cure for those who are not. The more likely scenario—that the student's limitations are not nearly so serious as he believes—requires the sensei to take a different approach. By refusing to cater to them, the sensei's presumed indifference, in fact, is a form of respect. He has a fundamental belief in the student's ability to rise to the challenges of budo practice. Unless there are serious troubles (the kind that, as we've already noted, should preclude a person from entering the martial arts in the first place until they are addressed), the path of the budo is sufficiently wide to walk for all of us. In expecting his students to do just that, the sensei expresses a respect for their potential.

Rather than becoming angry, dejected, or defensive about this, the student should be delighted and excited about learning from such a person. If you look around at a healthy dojo, you are apt to see students who are doing just that.

It is not by accident that in our discussion of what makes a good sensei, we have shifted the focus onto his students. In the end, while the sensei can be evaluated to some extent by his skills and teaching abilities, his final worth is determined by his *deshi*, his students. In this sense, a teacher of the budo is like a craftsman. Like the folk artists who make pottery or work with wood, the sensei must turn out a product that requires years to develop. He never settles for second-rate methods or shortcuts. If ever he makes changes in the way he approaches his work (and he does; all good teachers grow and refine themselves as part of the teaching process), it is only after long experience allows him that freedom. The sensei also takes pride in what he produces. For the potter, his finest work may be a rustic tea bowl or an exquisite jar. The master carpenter reaches his own zenith as a craftsman with a perfectly fitted joint, a building that will last far beyond his own life. The budo sensei's creation is in the forging of a mature budoka who can, in turn, express his personality and unique creativity through his art. The sensei may be paid for his teaching, or he may do it for the sheer love of his budo. His real reward, though, comes in the form of his students, who carry on the traditions in their own turn. And if they are not as faithful as Ono Tetsutaro, sitting graveside, keeping their teacher's spirit company through the storm, at least they will honor him by making what he has taught an integral part of their lives.

9

What's in a Name?

"What's in a name?" ponders Romeo. In the case of the rose he used an example, I don't really know. In others, however . . . Take for instance this one: Shinmen Miyamoto Musashi Fujiwara no Genshin.

Shinmen is a *myoji*, or family name, that of his father's side. It also appears in marriage documents from the family's home province with the notation of the alternative pronunciation, Niimi. His father's full name was Shinmen Munisai no suke Nobutsuna. Shinmen is a name Musashi's father was granted by a minor *daimyo* of Harima, the lord of Takeyama Castle, Shinmen Iga no kami Sudeshige. According to the *Niten-ki*, an anecdotal biography of Musashi that was compiled by some of his disciples after his death, the lord granted the name after Musashi's father defeated Yoshioka Shozaemon, a martial arts instructor of the shogun Ashikaga Yoshiaki (1537–1597). Before they were given the name Shinmen, Musashi's family name was Hirada. Hirada Shokan, who was Musashi's grandfather, had married into the family of the Iga daimyo; his wife was Sudeshige's daughter.

Are you confused yet? Hold on, it gets more interesting. It is typical of this mysterious martial artist that for reasons we'll never know, Musashi dropped the Shinmen name while he was still a boy. He adopted a surname that reflected the ancestral home—in a roundabout way to be sure, as we shall see shortly—of his mother's family, Miyamoto. Even in this name change there is another puzzle. Musashi was actually born in the Miyamoto neighborhood of the town of Ohara, located in Mimasaka Province, now part of the prefecture of Okayama. He insisted all his life, however, that he was from another village of the same name, the Miyamoto in the province of Harima, now Hyogo Prefecture. Furthermore, while Musashi's birth mother, Omasa, was from the Ohara Miyamoto neighborhood, she did not raise him. She died not long after giving birth. Musashi's father remarried, and it was this woman, Yoshiko, who raised Musashi. When he was still quite young, his parents—or more accurately, his father and stepmother—divorced. For some reason, Musashi left with his stepmother, to live in the Miyamoto village of Harima. Unwilling to admit it, or maybe unsure of where he was even born, a young man raised under circumstances that sound more like the plot of a bad soap opera than anything else might be forgiven for some of the eccentricities he later developed. It was not an auspicious beginning, to say the least. The beginnings of Musashi's genealogy, however, are far from such mystery. He came, as the saying goes, "from good stock."

Musashi's paternal ancestors were descended from the Akamatsu clan. The Akamatsu traced their lineage back to an early Imperial prince, Sanehira, who constructed the Sayo Castle in Harima in the middle of the twelfth century. The Akamatsu lived in the fortress until 1577 when, despite its name (*Sayo* means "a critical refuge"), the warlord Hideyoshi

Toyotomi attacked the castle and captured it. Musashi was born six years after that assault, in 1583 or, as the *Niten-ki* puts it, "in the third month of the year of *kanoe-saru*, the tenth year of Tensho." *Kanoe-saru* refers to the astrological/elemental cycle by which years were recorded in old Japan, a system based upon much older Chinese sources. *Kanoe* indicates that the year fell within the realm of metal in the five-part Taoist cycle of elements (fire, wood, water, earth, and metal). *Saru* means it was the Year of the Monkey. Tensho is the *nengo*, or name, chosen by the emperor at that time to describe his reign. The Tensho era was from 1573 to 1592.

The specific branch of the Akamatsu clan from which Musashi was descended in Harima counted among their direct ancestors the writer and poet Minamoto Morofusa (1003–1079). The Minamoto were a family related to the Murakami-Genji line, one of the families from which all the emperors of Japan have been chosen. The first of Musashi's ancestors to have used the name of Akamatsu was Akamatsu Suefusa (*ca.* A.D. 1060–1119). It was Suefusa who oversaw the construction of a castle in Harima, one he christened *Shirahata*, or roughly translated, "The White Fortress of Firm Resolution." An entry into documents associated with the building of the castle notes that Suefusa's ancestors had lived in the area for more than three centuries when he built the castle.

The Akamatsu were officially granted legal domain over the lands of Harima in 1333 when Akamatsu Norimura (A.D. 1287–1350) was the head of the family. Norimura answered a plea from the Imperial Prince Morinaga to come to the aid of the emperor. Or, more accurately, *one* of the emperors. There were at least two who were seriously claiming the title, with a few more entered into the race on the odd chance something might happen to one or both of the favorites. It was in the first half of the fourteenth century when the line of Imperial succession became contested. A powerful warrior family, the Hojo, challenged the rule of the emperor, Go-Daigo. The Hojo advanced a case for putting their own emperor into the court. Their claim led to a *Nancho*, or "Northern Court," and a *Hokucho*, or "Southern Court." (If you're interested, the Imperial line that continues today is from the Northern Court.) The Nambokucho War in Japan in the early fourteenth century was fought to decide which would prevail. Go-Daigo's son, Morinaga-shinno (1308–1335) asked Norimura, Musashi's ancestor, to join in the fight against the Hojo usurpers. Norimura responded—probably because he was a fervent disciple of Buddhism (he is sometimes referred to in historical records by his religious name, Nyudo Eishin)—and Morinaga, who sought his help, was a chief administrator of several temples, including the one at Mount Hiei.

Norimura met the Hojo general Nakatori on the outskirts of Kyoto and defeated him. The lands of Harima were a part of his reward. Such matters in Japan were at this time, shall we say, "fluid" at best. Within a few years and without any official explanation, the reward was rescinded by the Imperial Court. Akamatsu Norimura was left with no land other than that where his Sayo Castle sat. Consequently, he had no fields or rice that could be taxed, no way of making a living. Infuriated by this, he joined the anti-Go-Daigo forces, headed by Ashikaga Takuji (1305–1358). He was an implacable foe of the Go-Daigo regime for the rest of his life.

Musashi was descended from a son of Norimura's, Akamatsu Sadanori (*ca.* 1300–1356). Sadanori's elder brother, Akamatsu Norisuke (1312–1371) succeeded their father as head of the Akamatsu clan. Like his father, Norisuke was deeply committed to his religious faith. Instead of following the way of the warrior, he became a priest at the Mount Hiei temple. It was not until the onset of the Nambokucho War that, at the urging of the temple's chief priest, Norisuke took up the sword. He later served as the governor of Harima. As for Akamatsu Sadanori, who was Musashi's direct ancestor, little is known except that he made numerous improvements to the fortress built by his father, Norimasa, at Himeji. Later, these same fortifications were taken over by Hideyoshi, who used them as the foundation for the White Heron Castle, still standing and the most famous castle in Japan. So while he is popularly depicted in movies and stories as something of a country bumpkin, it is clear—well, maybe *clear* would not be your first choice of words at having waded through all those names and dates and stuff—but at least it is provable that Musashi's heritage was aristocratic. The Shinmen/Hirata family had suffered the misfortunes of wars and rebellions and politics by the era of his birth. But, coming from a prominent branch of the Akamatsu clan, they must have been regarded as more than ordinary peasants.

Musashi's connection with the Fujiwara family, another part of his name, is difficult to document reliably. The Fujiwara, like the Akamatsu, were among the most renowned clans in all of Japanese history. Great old families in the United States like to trace their roots to the *Mayflower*. In Europe, genealogies go back to early kings or rulers. The Fujiwara? They trace their ancestry to a god. The first Fujiwara was supposedly Ame no Koyane no mikoto, a Shinto deity present, according to the *Kojiki* (the "Book of Ancient Matters") at the very creation of Japan. While the *Niten-ki*, the biographical account of Musashi's life, is more reliable than the *Kojiki*, it has its limitations. It does not mention anything at all about a Fujiwara in Musashi's ancestry, even though the name is engraved on his tombstone. It is unlikely, however, that either Musashi or any of his ancestors would have fraudulently concocted a familial relationship with the Fujiwara, for at least two reasons. One, they probably did not have to. The Fujiwara was an enormously large family at that time. They were so numerous in the city of Kyoto alone that by the thirteenth century, they had to append their names to prevent chaos in making identification. The Kyoto Fujiwara referred to themselves, then, as the Nijo-Fujiwara ("Second Street Fujiwara"), Sanjo-Fujiwara ("Third Street Fujiwara"), and so on, based upon the boulevards where they lived. Rural members of the clan would combine one written character from their native area with another reading, usually with a variant pronunciation, of the kanji for "Fujiwara." The Fujiwara of Sakata town, for instance, took the *sa* of Sakata and added *to*, an alternate reading of the *fuji* of Fujiwara. So Sato, Kato, Endo; all these common Japanese names can conceivably have roots and a connection with the Fujiwara clan. Musashi's family could have rightfully claimed a link through any of these, or numerous others from whom they might have been descended.

The second reason it is not likely Musashi ginned up a fake connection with the Fujiwara was that deception about one's past has never been all that easy in Japan. Within less than a month of his birth, Musashi's parents would have been required by law to register his name in a *koseki*, a constantly updated census that was a part of the extensive record keeping maintained in each fiefdom. Feudal Japan was often less the land of the gallant, sword-swinging samurai (as it is so often depicted) as it was a massive bureaucracy. The tentacles of bureaucrats were wrapped like duct tape around nearly every aspect of life in old Japan. Rulers, from local village heads to daimyo to the shogun himself, all had a stake in knowing what was going on among the populace. Any sign of an uprising or political discontent could be detected in an examination of travel papers, sales of merchandise, or the dispensation of property.

Then, too, such magnificent piles of paperwork as were produced by a bureaucracy like feudal Japan's kept a lot of people employed. A great many samurai did the old nine-to-five routine as bean counters or tax collectors or scribes. Their mundane tasks, while not exactly reeking of derring-do, at least kept the fiefdom solvent economically and politically. At any rate, the records kept by most families, as well as by the local government officials, usually contained sufficient evidence of where one came from. To be less than honest about genealogy was not a good idea in a climate where most family histories were a matter of public record. When fanciful tales were whipped up about a family history, it was usually for political purposes among the upper classes, who would have tortuous family trees connecting far-flung "fourth cousins, twice removed" to get the desired result. So it is entirely reasonable to acknowledge Musashi's link to the Fujiwara that is found in the name on his grave. It is a connection with nobility that, along with his ancestral kinship to the Akamatsu, make his past as impressive as many of the great samurai of Japan.

Musashi's given name is the one by which he is best known. Yet it is not one he was known by at all until he was an adult. Before he was the Musashi, the lone victor (he might have been accompanied by a whole gang of supporters) in the romantic battle at Ganryu Island (which may or may not have occurred) where he defeated Sasaki Kojiro (who may or may not have existed), he was plain old Bennosuke. The name means "an assistant to learning." The -*suke* suffix, which means "to assist," but which carries the connotation of a stalwart "there-for-you" kind of guy, is a common one for men's names during this period. Bennosuke is a *yomyo*, also called a *domyo*; both mean a "childhood name." Yomyo were traditionally given to children within a week or so of their birth. For commoners, the yomyo usually sufficed for the rest of their lives. Males of the samurai class were often given a second name at about the age of six, as well as a third at a "coming of age" ceremony when they were around fifteen.

The second name a male member of the samurai caste received was his *jitsumyo*, or "formal name." Musashi's was Genshin. It means "a protector of nobility." In accordance with customs that went far back into Japanese history (as well as in the history of many cultures where personal names were thought to possess a certain spiritual power), a man's formal name was almost never used, even by his own family. The jitsumyo was usually connected to a clan name. In Musashi's case, he was named Fujiwara no Genshin, or the "Protector of the Noble House of Fujiwara." Not only was the jitsumyo rarely used, after a man's death it became one form of an *imina*, or "posthumous name," and was confined primarily to the written form when describing the deceased.

From his early adolescence, Musashi's popular name, the one by which he was called by friends and neighbors, was Takezo. This was a *zokumyo* (also called a *kenmyo* or *tsusho*). *Take* is a way of pronouncing the word for "martial." *Zo* as a suffix means "possessor." Since Musashi fought his first duel—killing Arima Kibei of the Shinto school of swordsmanship when he was only thirteen—the zokumyo seems appropriate.

And so where did the name "Musashi" come from? It is an alternate pronunciation for the characters used to write "Takezo." There is no record of when he changed the pronunciation of his name. But by his early adulthood, it was the one he used. This custom of changing the pronunciation of one's name was quite common in Japan at that time, and it is still done often there today. For instance, Musashi's birth mother, Omasa, had changed her name before he was born from the original, which was Masana.

Musashi is also known by the name Niten, or "Two Heavens." Niten is a *geimei*, or "art name." Artists of all kinds have frequently used geimei to sign their works. In some cases, this can drive historians and art collectors nearly mad. The *ukiyo-e* artist Hokusai Katsushika, for example, used over fifty different names for himself during his career. Some swordsmiths appear to have created a new signature geimei with nearly every other blade they forged. Niten Doraku is Musashi's *homyo*, or formal Buddhist name. It can be translated as "Enjoying the Way of Two Heavens," or "Two Heavens Enjoying Life." Musashi's homyo was given to him by the priest Shunran, at the Taisho Temple on Mount Tatsuta in Higo Province (today, Kumamoto Prefecture) while he was pursuing his studies of Buddhist scripture.

Finally, when Musashi died in 1645, he received one final name, an *okurina*, or posthumous Buddhist title. Musashi left this world as Myojin-dono Daiunshu Godaikoji, the "Wondrous Personage, His Excellency who Parted the Clouds and Revealed the Five Oceans." A classy title on which to go out, no?

And so, to answer Romeo's question of what's in a name—in the case of Shinmen Miyamoto Musashi Fujiwara no Genshin, a lot.

10

Nangyodo

The Way of Hardship

There is a significant difference between softness and weakness.

—Itto Ittosai Kagehisa

A couple of summers back, I was at an ethnic festival, one featuring various aspects of different nations and cultures. I noticed in the program that Japan was going to be represented in part by some martial arts demonstrations, so I went to the stage to watch. What I saw was a group of people performing something akin to aikido. Notice I said "something akin"—because what they were doing was not any kind of aikido I had ever seen. At best, it might have been some kind of undistinguished offshoot. It was one of those versions that disdain the more rigorous facets of aikido. It favored instead metaphysical tricks and a sort of muddled philosophy, the central precept of which appeared to be, given the narration of the event, the notion that if we all just had good thoughts, the world would be a nicer place. I had no particular quarrel with this concept. I do take exception, though, to those who are not doing it much at all but who wish to leech off the name of that art by calling their activities "aikido."

Now of course we all know that one person's aikido may be another person's "that's a load of garbage." The modern martial Ways, like aikido, karate-do, etc., have a wide range of representation. Approaches to them are varied. If you come to a judo exhibition expecting to see Olympic-caliber athletes going at it in a competition, and instead you are presented with a demonstration of the old *koshiki no kata* of judo, you might be tempted to scoff, "That's not judo." You would be narrow-minded in your assessment. The long, low stances of some Japanese forms of karate look different from the more compact, upright postures of the Okinawan versions of the art. Calling one the "real thing" while denying that others may have legitimacy is not supportable by the facts. Modern budo are, by their very structure and intent, broadly interpreted and executed. That is not to say, however, that they are infinitely elastic in their nature. What I saw at that ethnic fair was stretching the boundaries of the definition.

The group's demonstration began with a rambling explanation of the mystical forces that are the principles of their art. Then they proceeded to demonstrate some of those. At one point, the leader held the microphone with one hand and threw his opponents with the other, which might be a handy ability for the egregiously poor karaoke performer to possess, but which should also give you some idea of the kind of energy and spirit involved. In another part of the demonstration, a student was supposed to make an open-hand strike to the forehead of another. But the recipient of the attack was flustered. So the "attacker" thoughtfully and kindly allowed his strike to peter out somewhere off to the side of his intended target's shoulder. Both giggled sheepishly, then tried again. When anyone in the demonstration was thrown, their falling made almost no sound, no more than a child would have in executing a somersault. Sure, skillful *ukemi* (falling methods) can be slick; those who are really good at it make it look and sound almost effortless. In this case, though, it seemed almost as if those falling were throwing themselves. I shook my head a couple of times, wondering if my hearing had suddenly gone bad. (It hadn't.)

I have seen good demonstrations of aikido, from a number of different "styles" of the art that have evolved since Morihei Uyeshiba distilled it halfway through the last century. I understand there is no single and definitive way of doing it. Even so, I could not help but wonder what Uyeshiba would have thought of that demonstration. I wondered too, what he would think of those demonstrating. Some of them were seriously overweight. Most were so poorly trained and disciplined that they stumbled and hesitated when doing even simple, basic techniques. It was not, even by charitable standards, aikido. It was something masquerading as aikido. Of course, those people demonstrating were not deliberately deceiving the audience. No doubt they had been taught—as had their teacher, in all likelihood—that the things they were doing constituted a legitimate example of aikido as a budo form. Indeed, in their introduction they mentioned kindness toward others, etiquette, and perseverance in training—all hallmarks of budo, and, I'm sure, all sincere goals in their own lives. So it was particularly saddening to realize their chances of finding much meaning in the budo are small. They are lacking a critical element. Their approach to the budo has no *nangyo*, no "impetus of hardship," about it. To put it a bit more bluntly, they don't have enough violence in their training.

Now this may seem an odd criticism. Martial arts, especially their popular conception among the general public, appear to be long-suffering from just the opposite. On cable TV is the frequent spectacle of "Full-Contact Submission Kickboxing Death Matches," or something like that. In many schools of karate and other arts, what predominates are classes directed at beating the stuffing out of someone. Lip service is paid to the philosophical or moral elements of the martial arts. But that's about as far as it goes. Not enough violence in the martial arts scene today? That's like saying National Public Radio needs more somnolent on-air talent, isn't it? Well, yes. To some extent. Admittedly, the serious budoka generally ignores these almost cartoonish incarnations and looks for a more productive balance in his training. Yet in doing so, he needs to be careful not to tilt too far away from violence. Just as the macho displays of havoc and brawling are dangerously tipped in favor of the physical, lopsided too are those arts or approaches to those arts—like the version of aikido I saw—weighted too heavily on the side of the intellectual or the spiritual.

To better demonstrate what I'm talking about, consider the meanings of two words drawn from the theology of Buddhism: *jiriki* and *tariki*. They describe two distinct ways by which the faithful of Buddhism seek enlightenment. For some sects of Buddhism, enlightenment—or a release from the illusions of the world which, according to Buddhist thought, are the root of suffering—is attained through the grace of a divine act or some other miraculous event. These sects embrace the notion of tariki. A good way to translate it is "power gained effortlessly." For other forms of Buddhism, however, enlightenment comes through hard work on the part of the adherent, through meditation or various religious exercises. These sects are examples of jiriki, or, again to put it bluntly, "the hard way."

In the budo, we have our own approaches to enlightenment, or to that combination of physical talent, awareness, and spiritual equanimity we think of when we picture the most expert of practitioners. Martial artists of the distant past who attained a breakthrough in their search for mastery through miraculous events are the stuff of many legends. Aizu Hyuga no kami Iko (1452–1538) secreted himself in a cave in what is now Miyazaki Prefecture, in southern Japan, fasting and praying and receiving a divine revelation that led to his creation of the Kage ryu of swordsmanship. Later on, the Kage ryu became the basis for the Shinkage ryu, which has a section of the kata in its curriculum that supposedly were inspired by the lessons imparted by mountain goblins. The foundation of the Togun ryu is credited to the intervention of a deity enshrined on the mountain Myogisan, who gave secrets of strategy to Kawasaki Kaginosuke. In all these instances, inspiration came from an outside, supernatural force that showed up at just the right moment to bless the recipients with "the good stuff," through the aegis of tariki.

Morihei Uyeshiba's life is chockablock full of tariki. One of the best-known tales of his life was the time, in 1927, when a kendo instructor with the Japanese Army was visiting him, apparently asking for instruction. They argued about something. The dispute grew so intense the kendo teacher took up a bokken and swung at Uyeshiba. He was, goes the story, unable to even touch Uyeshiba, who whirled about the room, deftly dodging every strike, until the attacker finally gave up, dropping to the floor in exhaustion. Uyeshiba, unable to explain even to himself how he had managed to evade the sword, went out into his garden. There he was suddenly enveloped in a heavenly light that filled him with a spirit of love and harmony for all humankind.

I always wondered, hearing this story, what kind of kendo instructor it was who ran so completely out of breath he could not even stand up after making these attacks. Maybe part of Uyeshiba's miraculous skills were in being able to rob his attacker of the kind of stamina for which kendoka are justly famous. Whatever, Uyeshiba's ability to avoid the attacks came just before the divine light swept him up. It was a moment of tariki, followed by the illumination (in this case, literally) that is nearly always cited in his creation of aikido. Now, a point here is worthwhile mentioning: In these cases of tariki, it is relevant to remember that such inspirations, whether we believe the stories behind them uncritically or not, did *not* come out of the blue. Aizu Iko may have been meditating in a seashore cave when he was struck by the illumination that generated the Kage ryu; Uyeshiba might have been sitting around talking when he unceremoniously went into action against the kendo teacher. But neither of them had been slacking off for the many years before these strange events occurred. Their moments of tariki came after decades of long and hard practice. If you have read the novelization of Eiji Yoshikawa's epic, *Musashi*, you may have noticed one of the author's humorous ironies about Miyamoto Musashi. The young Musashi is constantly in search of some mysterious and miraculous secret of swordsmanship, roaming the countryside to find it, hoping for a tariki moment. He never seems to grasp that the real secrets he is discovering in his travels are not coming through the intercession of gods or goblins, but through hard daily training and meeting life head-on. That is because such efforts are the only way the principles of the budo can be grasped. They are mastered not through a physically transcendent moment of inspiration. They are not tariki. They are the result of jiriki. And so the path to them is one of *nangyodo*, or "the way of hardship."

The nangyo—the "difficulties" or "hardship" of the budo—comes in all sorts of forms. There are the special training sessions of midwinter and in the heat of summer. There are instructor-training programs that test the endurance and patience of advanced students. Testing in some budo is rigorous, and full of anxiety that is, in itself, a kind of hardship. All of these in their own ways work the same way as a sculptor's tools. They serve to chisel and chip and grind away all that is extraneous. If there is a weakness within, these harsh aspects of training highlight it so it can be taken out. The process of nangyodo is, like all elements of the budo that have any meaning or value, eliminative. One begins with all sorts of unnecessary weight and shape that have no worth or merit. When all that has been taken away, what is left is the form of the mature budoka.

While all these methods incorporated into budo training have their place, none of them can replace the most elemental form of hardship and struggle—grappling with another human being—that is so essential to the production of the martial artist. It does not matter so much in what manner this grappling is expressed. It can be empty-handed combat, as in judo or aikido or karate-do. Weapons may be involved, as with kendo. It does not matter *how* the struggle is joined so much as that the practitioner be willing to put his safety and comfort on the line. The spirit of the budo is achieved only through the threat of danger, the possibility of injury or death, and the awesome responsibility that one may inflict either of these on another.

Now look: I am not in any way suggesting we in the budo approach life like some kind of daredevils with a death wish. Or that we have to be caught up in a murderous frenzy in order to be serious about our practice at the dojo. I am adamant on one point, however. If we are not engaged in a personal encounter with violence and the dangers it implies, we are not doing budo. It is part of the genius of these arts that they have been designed in such a way that they are practiced with all sorts of safeguards. Protective gear, as in the case of kendo, or rules against some kinds of strikes or throws or locks, as in the empty-handed forms, allow for violent energies to be exercised and polished. The classical koryu martial arts are particularly clever in their use of wooden weapons and in the teaching of reactions and responses that allow their members to make attacks at full strength and speed, and stop them just before contact, or in ways that reduce the threat somewhat. Yet even with these protections, we can and do get hurt. It cannot be avoided. If you want to learn to kill or incapacitate someone, to develop the mentality that will allow you to face mortal danger with coolness and equanimity, you cannot do that sitting in a chair and reading a book about it. You have to go where it is and to be a part of it.

No philosophical writings or intellectual discourse can instill in the judoka hurtling through the air the proper reactions to apply a correct and timely breakfall. He must *feel* it, must know that if he does not relax and fall properly, his injuries could well be grave. Lectures, no matter how inspired, will never encourage the karateka to shift and counter as quickly as will the threat of his senior's incoming kick. He knows that if the threat is not met as it should be, that he will be injured. He knows this in an entirely different way than does the observer who is watching the action and who has some theoretical understanding of the mechanics of karate's movements. These sorts of lessons are difficult to learn. They must be part of a very carefully instituted program, beginning with the basics and gradually working up to the more sophisticated and complex arenas of the art. They must be introduced so slowly that the student is not prematurely thrust into a situation for which he has no experience.

If he is, and he is hurt as a result, he is likely to quit or to shy away from the kind of training that caused the injury. Having said that, however, we must still face the obvious truth of the budo. Lessons of this sort encountered there can be painful and frightening. But they are lessons absolutely vital if one is ever to grasp the meaning of the martial Ways.

It has always been this way. Budo have always been approached through nangyodo. The late Masatoshi Nakayama of the Japan Karate Association recalled in an interview that often his forearms became so sore and swollen from blocking his classmates' attacks in the early days of the JKA that he could not sleep at night. The Americans, mostly servicemen during the Occupation of Japan who came into contact with judo's Kyuzo Mifune, tend to remember a kindly, perpetually smiling old gentleman. If they had the opportunity to get out on the mat and train with Mifune, the last of judo's tenth-dan, they told different stories. Even into his seventies, Mifune threw opponents hard enough to knock them unconscious when they hit the mat, even though they were adept at taking judo's falls. Uyeshiba's disciples have recalled that just months away from his death, his grip was strong enough to leave bruises on their wrists when he grabbed them.

"Yeah, I know," an old kendo teacher once told me, "it's always the way: the geezers like me always talk about how much harder it was back in the old days. But I'll tell you what. I was there in the dojo and I saw guys get hit so hard on the forehead part of their *men* [padded head protector], they went down to their knees. I saw shinai [split bamboo staves used as mock swords] splinter when they hit against a guy's *wrist*. Kendo's never been gentle. But in those days, it *hurt*."

So from the experiences of these old-timers, should we infer that "real" training in the budo should be a regular bloodbath? If you are not sustaining serious injuries, is that a sign your training isn't worthwhile? If that were the case, you could count me out. I have collected the usual sorts of injuries over the years in my budo practice. I have hurt others, unintentionally and never very seriously. I've been fortunate, from both perspectives. If deliberately inflicting pain or courting it is the only way to reach the loftier heights of the martial arts, then I will have to be content to sit out the climb somewhere down around the base camp. I do not believe, though, that accepting the possibility of injury is tantamount to deliberately inflicting or enduring it. I do not believe violence in and of itself is a pathway to mastering the martial Ways. I am sure, however, that confronting violence, engaging in it through the conventions of budo training, is critical to mastery. Every form of the traditional Japanese *Do* have their own means of refining character. In the tea ceremony, the adherent's personality and character are shaped by an immersion into the aesthetics and practicalities of preparing tea. Conforming to the postures and movements, acquiring the expected attitudes— these shape the *chajin*, the "tea person." In the budo, character is built, in part, at least, through the medium of violence and struggle with others. It is constructed through the medium of nangyo. Without these elements—without the presence of nangyo, judo, aikido, and the other combative arts of Japan—the budo are no longer martial. They might be a Way of some kind. But they cannot be construed in any realistic form as *martial Ways.*

Most readers will know that the foundation of the modern martial Ways lies in the classical, battlefield arts of the era of the samurai in Japan. Their conversion, modification, and translation into forms more acceptable to the post-feudal world have been the subject of considerable debate. No matter how one feels about that evolution, there cannot be much disagreement in the proposition that these budo were formulated in no minor way as a means of spiritual and moral self-cultivation. To suggest that this is a goal that can be met by having the dojo strewn with broken bodies is absurd. On the contrary, if I saw people regularly injured in a class, it would be a compelling sign to me that this was one dojo where I did not want to join or even practice. (Likewise, a dojo where beginners are expected to train with the same intensity and be treated to the same behavior as the advanced students is also one from which I would immediately take my leave.) But the occasional bloody nose or cut lip; the sprain or bruise; all these and other relatively minor injuries are going to occur if the training is hard and sincere. They are a part of nangyo.

At the risk of repeating myself and hammering home a nail that is already securely in place, let's review: It is foolish to place oneself under the tutelage of an instructor who cannot control the violence in his dojo, or to participate in training where those controls seem unimportant or are unknown to members. The sensei's task is to regulate the pace and the nature of training so that a serious martial rigor is constantly maintained, without either slacking off or going over the edge into chaos. It is equally foolish to assume that if you are going to pursue the budo on a lifelong basis that you will never be hurt or frightened.

A final question remains. If violence is an accepted and expected part of following a martial Way, how can the student know if his dojo is really a place for learning budo, or if it is simply a glorified arena for violent pathologies to be expressed? What is the difference between a real dojo and a place that allows bullies and masochists free rein? The difference lies in the word nangyo itself. The character for *nan* means "that which is extremely difficult," or "bordering on the impossible." *Gyo* refers to a "busy place," or a crossroads, a place where many people come and go. What we can infer then, is that gyo implies a step of learning along the Way. It is a part of the journey, not a destination. Gyo is about the process of becoming, and not the completion itself. In the budo, violence is not an end, not a goal worth pursuing for its own sake. Instead, it is a part of the path necessary to walk in order to get to where we want to go. If you keep this distinction in mind, it is clear how violence can be determined to be an end in a training hall, or a means.

The people who employ violence for its own sake in our culture are, unfortunately, numerous. Maybe not so numerous as the pessimist would like to believe. The twenty-first century probably compares well to other times and other civilizations in that regard. Comparing the carnage of the gladiatorial rings of ancient Rome with the football gridiron is a popular metaphor inevitably meant to cast our age in a gruesome light. The comparison is ridiculous, though. Neither do car-crashing, bullet-spraying video games serve as modern-day equivalents of bear-baiting and public dueling and other brutalities from earlier periods in our history. Even so, we live in an age where planned violence, from the boxing ring to full-contact sporting contests, is not uncommon. The goals for these events may be financial, or for personal satisfaction, or some other motive. They are not the goals of the budo. While we may share a connection with these, involving ourselves in the process of violence, with "fighting" of one kind or another, our intent is— or at least it should be—markedly different. For the serious budoka, nangyodo is a part of a journey. It is a road that is designed to take us beyond making a buck or becoming a champion. It is a road that has nowhere been more succinctly described than by Jigoro Kano, writing about his hope for judo as a martial Way:

> By training one in attacks and defenses, judo refines the body and the soul. It helps one make the spiritual essence of judo a part of his very core. In this way, we are able to perfect ourselves and create something of value to the world.

11

Mythic Origins of the Ninja

Trains in Japan are nicely suited to long, leisurely stretches of reading. The passenger is interrupted only by the girls who periodically sell box lunches and other snacks, and, if he chooses to take it in, the vista passing outside his window. Otherwise, it is quiet. The seats are comfortable, and traveling otherwise alone, a good book is a happy and welcome companion. Almost pathologically afraid of being caught under these circumstances without a book, I select with care when I am going to Japan. It has to be lightweight, a paperback by necessity then. But long enough to be savored slowly, page after page. Jonathan Raban's book, *Old Glory*, recounting his boat trip down the Mississippi, was among the first items packed in my bag when I got ready to go on my last trip. Travel books when one is traveling are particularly satisfying. The sense of estrangement and loneliness that are a part of solo travel are always assuaged to some extent for me by reading an author's similar account of being a "stranger in a strange land." And I was that. So Raban's book was going to take me through the middle of Shiga Prefecture, on my way from Nara up to the northern part of central Japan. But just as I was leaving the *ryokan*, the inn where I had been the guest of the owner, he pressed a thick binder into my hands. A Buddhist layman with a deep interest in his faith and in the early history of Japan, Nakanishi-san had been up with me until the small hours of the night before. We'd talked of this and that, and now he had a parting gift for me.

"It is a translation I did of an old book about Shiga," he said. "Since you're going through there, I thought you might like to read it."

I was taking the train from Nara up to the northern part of central Japan, passing through the center of Shiga Prefecture. While it sits in the middle of the Omi Basin, home of Japan's largest lake, Biwa, mountains surround all sides of Shiga. There is the Nosaka Range to the north, the Ibuki Mountains to the east, the Suzuka on the southeast, and to the west, between Shiga and Kyoto, the forbiddingly steep Mount Hiei dominates the skyline.

Shiga was once known as Omi Province. The three great highways of the eastern part of Japan—the Nakasendo, the Hokuriku, and the Tokai—all converged here, so it was a center for commerce. The sixteenth-century warlord, Oda Nobunaga, came from Omi. So, in the nineteenth century, did the painter-poet, Kiitsu. But the history of Shiga goes much further back than Japan's feudal era. The mountains all around are home to stone monoliths and weird circles of rock, like a smaller version of the formations at Stonehenge.

Before Shiga was even called Omi, it was, six thousand years ago, a center of civilization for the Jomon culture. The Jomon was a prehistoric civilization that produced mysteriously beautiful sculptures of wide-eyed people, their mouths shouting in big, silent "Os." Recent archaeological digs in Shiga have almost completely revised earlier concepts of the Jomon. Once they were considered simple hunter-gatherers. Aside from their pottery, the sculptures that somehow look more modern than the most modern of art today, and clay baskets decorated with rope patterns, they were supposed to have been primitive at best. Evidence of large, elaborate wooden buildings and other clues found at the end of the twentieth century point, however, to a civilization far more advanced. It seems the Jomon, named after their enigmatic pottery, may have been a kind of Japanese version of the Celts, steeped in their own lore and nature-worshipping beliefs, but technologically more sophisticated than anyone thought. And so Shiga is an ancient place, even by the hoary standards of Japanese history.

I read Raban's account of his passage down the Mississippi until the train crossed over the border into Shiga Prefecture; then, knowing I would feel guilty if I did not, I took out the binder and opened it and began to read the typewritten pages. It was Nakanishi-san's translation of *Omi no Kuni Yochishi*, "An Account of the Places and Land of Omi Province." It was fascinating. Entertaining as the account of a journey down the Mississippi had been, I soon forgot all about it. Turning page after page of the translation, I was lost. An hour passed before I knew it. The sky had been gray all morning outside the train window. Now, as I looked up from the binder, a wet autumn rain began to fall. Those long, ragged veils of mist dangled down in the valleys between the mountains as they do throughout the countryside of Japan at that time of year. It gave the passing scenery an eerie quality—dark, thick forests, with only the occasional little hamlet popping into and out of view instantly as the train passed by. If you could overlook the electric lines and a few other distractions, it could have been the Japan of centuries ago. Perhaps the book, devoted to old myths and occurrences supernatural and otherwise that had unfolded there long in the past, heightened my perspective. Stories about mountain goblins and haunted temples and some intriguing hints about another of Shiga's most renowned creatures: the ninja.

Few characters from the East have captured the imagination of the West more than the ninja. Presented as black-cloaked Japanese James Bonds, their arts and crafts and image have been the focus of huge interest for Westerners. There is almost certainly more interest in the ninja, in fact, in say, Pittsburgh, than there is in Nara. Erstwhile confederacies of "modern ninja" pursue their versions of "ninjutsu" in training halls dedicated to the art, throughout the U.S. It may not be a coincidence that, in contrast to all this enthusiasm, there is virtually no serious scholarship about ninja published outside of Japan. Go to an American bookstore and look in the martial arts section, and you will likely find at least a dozen books on the subject. Open them, however, and you will find almost none contains any primary sources cited in their bibliographies. What few references there are will be secondary, English sources, and most of those questionable. That's not my problem. And I don't have any contention with those who want to practice whatever it is of their ninjutsu that suits their fancy. It is regrettable, though, that more aficionados of the ninja do not take the time to learn to read Japanese or to otherwise access scholarly Japanese sources. There are such books and papers. And then too, one sometimes comes across references to the ninja in the most unexpected places, as I did in the translation of Nakanishi-san's I was reading.

In the *Account of the Places and Land of Omi Province* was a brief overview of the legends that surround the origins of ninjutsu. That is understandable. Omi was home to some of the family groups that specialized in espionage and intelligence gathering in old Japan. With the intersection of major highways and the bustling commerce there, information was a plentiful commodity. The book presented—labeling them all plainly, it is important to note, as nothing more than folk tales and *not* authentic history—the generative accounts of various systems of ninjutsu from Omi.

The Koga systems of ninjutsu (there were nearly thirty of them, according to records of the province) traced their ancestry back to the mythic era of the gods of Japan. Susano-o no mikoto was the earthly though still divine offspring of the two progenitors of Japan itself, Izanagi and Izanami. A hell-raiser from his earliest years, Susano-o wreaked such mischief he was eventually exiled by the other earthly deities who were roaming about Japan at that time. He matured in exile—and must have learned something of what it is deities were supposed to do with themselves. When he shows up again, in the *Kojiki*, Japan's collection of myths that explain this period, it was to embark on some high adventure. Susano-o set out to do battle with a gigantic, multi-headed reptile. (Most translations of the *Kojiki* call it a snake. Ethnologists speculate the better word might be something like "crocodile." There are no such animals in Japan and never have been, fossils indicate. So the appearance of a crocodile might hint at this myth's origination in another part of Southeast Asia.)

The battle with the reptile was joined, according to the myth, at the request of a couple who had lost all but one of their children to the beast. Think of it as a Japanese rendition of Beowulf meets Hydra. As an incentive to Susano-o, the couple offered their last child, a daughter named Kushinada-hime ("Wondrous Inada Princess"), to him in marriage. Before he went out to fight the multi-headed creature, Susano-o changed his fiancée into a "many-toothed close comb that he stuck in the august knot of his hair." With Kushinada-hime concealed, Susano-o attacked the snake, first luring him into a maze-like fence. There are, incidentally, many kata in classical schools of swordsmanship named after this "eight-fold fence," or *yaegaki*. Susano-o slaughtered the beast. In its tail he found a sword that was one of the three sacred regalia of Japanese Shinto. The Koga systems of ninjutsu, according to the book about Omi legends, credit Kushinada-hime with being the secret power that helped defeat the reptile, and she is considered their patron saint because of it. Concealed as a comb, she was hidden from the battle and yet right in the thick of the action. This was the ideal of the ninja as conceived by the Koga traditions—to be out of sight and yet at the heart of the conflict, working behind the scenes to ensure success.

There are several clues in what remains of the Koga systems of espionage that allude to their particular relationship with Kushinada-hime. Supposedly, there were references in their teachings to *kamikakure*: "hidden in the hair." And some of the *kamon* (family crests of families that have long resided in the Shiga region), like that of the Rokkaku clan of old Omi, for instance, are stylized depictions of a hair comb. This famous samurai clan was involved in many of the battles and intrigues of the imperial court during the fourteenth and fifteenth centuries. One can only guess they must have had several occasions to employ some of the secrets of the Wondrous Inada Princess.

To be sure, a number of arts, martial and otherwise, that come down to us from long-ago Japan describe divine or supernatural forces as the instruments of their founding. Just as the Koga methods of espionage credit a princess turned into a comb for their inspiration, another, the Iga systems of ninjutsu, go just as far back in detailing their own evolution. According to the account in the book of Omi legends, it was another episode detailed in the *Kojiki* that was the genesis of their traditions. The *Kojiki* tells about a schism that had formed between the heavenly deities and their earthly counterparts. The former watched down on the gods who were actually living in Japan at this time, and they were unhappy with what they saw. The earthly deities had been bickering and fighting among themselves; Japan was in a state of chaos. The situation became so dire, the heavenly gods dispatched a scout to get a clearer picture of the goings-on. The scout was a pheasant, Naki-me (or in some versions, Naka-me), who winged down from the heavens to reconnoiter. No sooner had he landed in a tree than he was spotted, however, by Ama-no-waka-piko. The latter had good reason to be worried about the appearance of a divine pheasant who was looking around carefully. Ama-no-waka-piko had himself been ordered by the heavenly deities to go to Japan to investigate. He had done so, but found he liked the neighborhood so well, he decided to defect. He was living happily in the fraternity house kind of shenanigans of mythic Japan. Fearful that his defection would be uncovered, he shot Naki-me with an arrow.

The bolt passed through the bird, then "shot up and through the heavens," piercing the sky as it flew. It was another god there, Taka-ki-no-kami, who found the arrow, covered in blood. He recognized it as one that had been bestowed upon Ama-no-waka-piko, when that deity was preparing for his trip to the earth. Furious, Taka-ki-no-kami hurled the arrow back down through the same hole it had torn in the sky on the way up. It struck Ama-no-waka-piko, killing him. "Such," notes the *Kojiki*, "is the origin of the saying 'beware the returning arrow.' "

The *ya no gaeshi*, or "returning arrow," is a very old Japanese expression, not used much anymore in Japan. In earlier times, it was an aphorism of warning, sort of like the more modern Japanese *bachi ga ataru*, or "watch out for your luck coming back to hit you." In the Iga tradition of ninjutsu, however, the returning arrow was adopted as a symbol. The pheasant Naki-me is given credit as their patron. The pheasant was, after all, sent out on a mission to gather intelligence. He was a spy. His names are variously given as Naki-me, which can be translated from very old Japanese as "listening to one's own cries," or Naka-me, meaning "a nameless one." It doesn't require much imagination to see where both of these could have a special significance to the ninja who dealt in "listening" and in tricking enemies into believing false information, as well as those who had to remain nameless in order to succeed at their tasks. There is as well an archaic expression in early Japanese literature about the "one-way errand of the pheasant." The phrase, of course, comes from this incident. Just as Naki-me died trying to complete his mission, he was supposed to have been a model for the ninja of Iga, who were expected to complete their assignments— even if it meant they would not come out alive.

According to legend, it was the warrior and spymaster Hattori Hanzo who founded the Iga traditions of espionage. Hattori was born in Mikawa, but his family's ancestral home had been in Iga Province, now part of Mie Prefecture, which was directly to the southeast of Omi. In the translation of the book, Hattori is mentioned, along with a story that linked him with a mysterious Chinese scholar. The tale has it that in 221 B.C., a physician named Hsu-fu came to Japan. (This would predate by many centuries any proven historical record of such a visit; remember, we're talking about legends here.) Hsu-fu was a Taoist, in search, as Taoists often are, of the elixir that would provide eternal life. He brought with him a retinue of six hundred men and women. From this band, so says one version of the legend, was created the Japanese nation. Understandably, few serious scholars would entertain this fabulous account. Historical records do acknowledge the existence of a visitor from China named Hsu-fu, or, as the characters for his name are read in Japanese, Jofuku. His grave is in Shingu, in Wakayama Prefecture; there are numerous shrines and temples dedicated to him as well.

While he was looking for eternal life, Jofuku brought with him a vast store of medicinal knowledge, along with fantastic abilities of wizardry. The book of Omi legends states it was this combination of science and arcane teachings that became the basis for the principles of ninjutsu, and that Hattori Hanzo was descended from Jofuku, or from one of those who came from China with him. The truth might be that Jofuku's name was fixed onto the origination stories of ninjutsu to give the system behind it an aura of importance and grandeur. To be sure, there is no verifiable lineage we can trace back to Jofuku. But when we are in the realm of myth, why not? If a venerable celestial wizard does not add prestige to your lineage, who would?

But if you couldn't exactly prove your ancestor was a Chinese master of the occult, how about claiming one's progenitor was the lord of one of Japan's most powerful families? A clan, like the Otomo, that pulled strings and manipulated political events in early Japan much the same way as the Borgia did in sixteenth-century Italy. While the connection between Hattori Hanzo and Jofuku is more fantasy than anything else, the secretive Hattori and the Otomo family have a common thread that gets more interesting the more you pull on it. The name Otomo itself may have meant something like "auspicious protector" in early Japanese. The Otomo, if we are to believe their history, were founded by a grandson of the Sun Goddess who accompanied her when she traveled to earth. At least slightly more supportable is evidence the Otomo were a distant branch of the imperial family who lived in and around the lands that are now Shiga Prefecture. From the sixth century until the ninth, the Otomo clan produced several political leaders who were also military men. Incidentally, more than a few of the Otomo of this period were poets as well. The literary works of Otomo no Yakamochi, Otomo no Tabito, and Otomo Kanamura are still read today in Japan.

Otomo no Hosoto was a strategist for the Soga, a family (really, it was more like a confederated tribe) that included Shotoku, an offspring of the Soga's leadership, still in his teens.

In the late sixth century, a power struggle erupted of the sort that would occur again and again in Japanese history. The Soga and the Monobe clans vied for the right to claim imperial succession. Looking at their land and political connections, their wealth and the size of the armies they were able to raise, the smart bet would have been on the Monobe. But somehow—exactly how has continued to elude historians—the Soga, backed by Otomo no Hosoto, emerged the victors. Young Shotoku was elevated to the status of regent, serving under the empress Suiko. Prince Shotoku is one of the towering figures of this epoch of Japanese history. He wrote a constitution that carved out the legitimacy of a ruler's supreme authority that would last in Japan for almost thirteen-hundred years. He adopted the Chinese calendar, along with encouraging the spread of Buddhism. He is responsible for instituting a centralized and bureaucratic government. Did Shotoku and his Soga clan benefit from behind-the-scenes machinations by the crafty strategist Otomo no Hosoto? There isn't any doubt there were assassinations, double-crossings, and double-dealings, and political intrigues of every sort going on in the struggle for political control in Japan at that time. So it is easy to see there might have been some espionage or counterintelligence activities, and Otomo is a natural suspect in anything like that. Whatever the truth, Otomo is often cited as being among the first of the agents we might think of as ninja today. And guess who could trace his ancestry back to Otomo no Hosoto? Hattori Hanzo, of course. Think about it. A warrior in the last half of the sixteenth century who participated in espionage for the Tokugawa shogun, who had come from an ancestor that could have been doing the same for an imperial regent in the sixth.

I closed the binder and looked out the rain-streaked train window, and thought about Hattori and Otomo, both of whom had lived in the countryside that was passing by outside my window.

Engaging stuff about which to speculate and upon which to let one's imagination wander—yes, even though it was only a book of legends and some facts that may have been open to dispute. Like a lot of what passes for "information" about the ninja today. The modern popular depictions of ninja are—to put it gently—inaccurate. To put it more bluntly, they are to the reality of Japan during the feudal era what Cinderella is to life in Europe's Middle Ages. However, there is also no doubt that those popular depictions are just that: popular. As I noted earlier, there are places proposing to teach the arts of the ninja in nearly every city of any size in the U.S. I have passed these schools in Kansas City or Tucson or Seattle, and wondered: How did a medieval Japanese spycraft come to inspire a stripmall rental space full of people clad in black, somersaulting, tossing about and whacking one another with odd weapons?

Whatever their motivations, I like to think the modern American ninjutsu students are not there believing they are studying some art with an unbroken linkage going back dozens of generations, keeping bright and hot the flame of secret agents of Japan's feudal cloak-and-dagger. (Kimono-and-sword?) Not so much as a sliver of documentation exists for nearly all the fantastic historical claims made about ninja. What little we do know of the ninja during the medieval period is intriguing, but hardly the stuff of camouflaged derring-do, acrobatics, and 007-type gadgets. Some members of the warrior class, like Hattori, specialized in espionage techniques. Among them, again like Hattori, were leaders who were able to organize spy networks, some of them sizable and complex. They engaged in intelligence gathering and other clandestine tasks as part of their duties to their daimyo. There were also ninja, most of them outside the samurai caste and not a few of whom were among Japan's criminal class, who worked for the highest bidder. They would have committed arson or kidnapping or terrorism and strong-arm for whoever paid them. A case might be made that such distinctions were morally moot. If I, as a samurai, steal into your house and kill your daughter to prevent her from marrying a political enemy of my lord, an arrangement that would weaken my lord's power, how is that any different than if I, as a blood-for-hire outlaw, sneak in and kill your daughter, acting on orders from a local business rival who wants to intimidate you?

No matter how we look at it, though, spying and skulking in the dark are never as romantic in reality, not in old Japan nor in our own age, than they might sound or look in movies or novels. More importantly, romanticizing the feudal period of Japan is anathema to understanding it. Myths and legends are never substitutes for solid and objective historical research. My own writing has often been aimed at stripping away fantasy about historical Japan and trying to get readers to understand what it was in reality. Feudal Japan (even more so, its history before that) was so different from our time and place as to form significant obstacles in getting to what the legends were about. Being able to uncritically accept the legends isn't going to help in navigating that path. That is not to say, however, that we should entirely and always discount the legendary. So much of the past of Japan's martial traditions are swirled with the mists of legend. Old stories can provide clues. Was it a crocodile that held the miraculous sword in its tail in the earliest versions of the *Kojiki*? If so, anthropologists can make some intelligent conjectures about the originations of the Japanese people. A plausible theory has arisen about another tale of the *Kojiki*. The Sun Goddess retreated to a cave, goes the account, and had to be lured out to save the people of Japan from the long, cold darkness that ensued. Geological evidence hints at a series of convulsive volcanic eruptions that rocked Japan a few thousand years back. Clouds of ash would have covered the sky for years, maybe long enough to have inspired a myth about a fickle deity who needed to be flattered into returning and bringing light and warmth with her. (See chapter 13 for more on this.)

Even if they are not historically accurate and factual in every way, the annals of legends about Omi Province have value for the glimpse they offer into the past of that part of Japan. And, I have to admit, they are worthwhile simply because they have the power to stir our imagination. I sat and read them and looked up every once in a while to take in the scenery. Shadowy forests, the steep hills cut by ravines threaded with streams that boiled and splashed over mossy boulders. These were the places where men like Hattori Hanzo walked, and where a well-aimed arrow could have been seen to pierce a pheasant and then the heavens, places where the mythic and the real could understandably become hard to separate. No, the records of Omi legends are not history. Still, there are worse ways to spend a rainy afternoon on a train in the mountains of Shiga.

12

To Blossom and to Scatter . . .

Flowers blossom and scatter. It is their blooming and scattering that is their essence.

—Giken Honda

When planning the construction of a dojo, there are, of course, priorities. Space must be sufficient for training, with ceilings high enough to accommodate any weapons if they are to be used. The floor is critical. If it is going to be matted, the underlying structure has to give some, but not too much, support. If it is wood, there must be some give as well, along with a smooth and level surface. Ventilation, dressing rooms, lighting— all these are of concern when drawing up blueprints. Pragmatism must often take precedence over aesthetics. That is why the *tokonoma* is a feature of the dojo sometimes neglected or ignored, even if the planners are aware of its function.

Some might argue, in fact, that the tokonoma, or alcove, has no place in a traditional dojo. If you have ever been in a

Japanese home, you have probably seen a tokonoma. It is a recessed space, designed to be the focal point of the room, where a scroll might hang, or some beautiful or significant object displayed. There are two stories to account for the development of tokonoma. One has it that such a special spot was needed when tatami mats began to be used throughout Japanese homes. Mats were once reserved for the head of the house or for other important people to sit. When, around the eleventh century, tatami began to be laid throughout the house, some designation of a superior position within the house was needed. The raised space of the tokonoma got its start in filling that need. The other theory states that, around the same time, Chinese paintings on silk scrolls became popular, and the alcove evolved as a space to display them. The tokonoma is a result of the *shoin* style of architecture that developed during the Fujiwara period (*ca.* 900–1100). But the dojo is modeled after the earlier *shinden* style of the Heian era (*ca.* 800–900) and so, argue some, an alcove does not belong in a martial arts training hall.

Certainly a tokonoma is not an architectural necessity in a dojo. Most of the dojo I have visited in Japan have them, but the majority of them are what are referred to as a "country style." These tokonoma are merely recessed sections of the front wall, without any of the features of the traditional alcove—like a pillar, or *tokobashira*, that are found in the formal tokonoma of a home, a hut, or place designed for the tea ceremony, for instance. In a simple dojo tokonoma, there might be a sword on a rack placed there, or a suit of armor. There might also be flowers arranged in the tokonoma space. Particularly in the West, and particularly in aikido dojo, we find these flowers in the dojo alcove. I suspect it started in aikido because the basis of ikebana (flower arranging) has at its roots a kind of votive offering at temple altars, and of all the modern martial Ways, aikido most closely identifies itself with Buddhist thought. Whatever the reason, and even though it may not be "traditional," I like the idea. I wish more dojo followed the practice.

As I said, it is easy to understand how such a space in the dojo might have to give way to the demands of designing a good training area. And later on, the tasks of teaching and maintaining the dojo are apt to take precedence over such apparently superficial matters (perceived as solely decorative) like the arranging and displaying of fresh flowers. That's reasonable; but neglecting to have fresh flowers in a dojo also risks contributing to the development of training places—we need not look far to find examples of these—that are physically healthy but lacking in soul. They are filled with enthusiastic practitioners who are learning well the outer, purely physical aspects of their art—yet something often seems to be missing, something unidentifiable or inexplicable in words. Perhaps it is noticeable only because of its absence. Some may deny this. But it is obvious many dojo are sensing it, and we can see that as they try to fill the gap. Today, much more than say, twenty years ago, dojo in the West are, for instance, celebrating *kagami biraki*, a part of the traditional Japanese New Year festivities. They may offer *misogi* (training exercises of a meditative and purifying nature). Dojo are also increasingly making or purchasing *kamiza*, adding these Shinto shrines to shelves at the front of their training hall, even though they may not be adherents to Shinto. All these appear fundamentally to be efforts at nurturing or reestablishing a spirit, an attitude, the matter of what we might call, for lack of a better term, the "soul" of the budo as a part of training.

I was taught that the arranging of flowers in the dojo alcove was a real and significant way to foster this soul of budo. It was partly, I suppose, because my sensei's wife was a chajin, a practitioner of the tea ceremony, and she arranged flowers as a part of that art, teaching me the basics of *chabana*, the specialization of flower arranging used in tea ceremonies. But I also had it impressed upon me that the flowers in the dojo were a glimpse into the essence of the budo, a reminder to be found in the blooming and the scattering of the petals that keep us focused on what it is, in the end, all about.

When I was attending an aikido seminar some years ago, the hosting teacher asked if I would put together an arrangement of flowers for the tokonoma. It wasn't difficult, even though I am not at all skilled in the art. The dojo was out in a rural area, surrounded by meadows that were waist-deep in the last of summer's daisies. I cut some and arranged them in a simple form. The teacher thanked me. "You need to show me how to do some of that stuff so I can do it myself," he said. Oh sure. Got a decade to spend on that? The comment is understandable. But it is roughly equivalent to someone walking into an aikido dojo and requesting the teacher there show him some of "that stuff" so he can go do it himself. Lest the reader believe that formal flower arranging is a skill that can be picked up by taking a couple of classes, a brief explanation of ikebana is in order.

Exactly like the budo, ikebana has its roots in Japan's classical age. Remember that while we in the West had a very short classical period during the heyday of Greek civilization, followed by a long romantic period that continues in many ways today, in Japan it was just the opposite. The romantic Heian era lasted not much more than a century, around A.D. 800. What followed was more than seven hundred years of classicism. What that meant, among other things, was that attention to form was critical to the artistic process. Thought, emotion, inspiration; these are expressed through the structure of the form. If the form was not correct, the motivation behind it was suspect as well. The classical approach to virtually all forms of artistic endeavor was remarkable in Japan. The medieval epoch there spawned an extraordinary growth in art, from the combative disciplines to the tea ceremony, from cooking methods to theater to calligraphy. The same was true for flower arranging. All were taught according to a correct and precise form, through the aegis of the *ryu*, the tradition or school, each with its own, distinguishable skills, curricula, and lore. The teacher of the ryu passed down its heart through the kata. Just as the arts of swordsmanship had their kata, ikebana developed its own forms. The member of an ikebana ryu learned to create compositions with flowers and other natural materials by emulating the model set by the teacher. The parameters of combative kata were set by the necessities of the battlefield. Ikebana kata took their generative impulse from an idealized version of nature. The dimensions and composition of an ikebana arrangement are a reflection of the aesthetics of beauty, consonant with native Japanese concepts and with Taoist sources that identify certain geometric configurations as decorous.

Ikebana ryu flourished (most are still intact) under the hands of hereditary headmasters, just as did martial ryu. Like the fighting man's combative ryu, ikebana schools also issued licenses that recognized varying levels of ability and gave the right to teach. Martial ryu and ikebana ryu share the intriguing convention of the *okuden*. Literally "hidden teachings," okuden are secrets zealously guarded by the individual ryu. They are, in many ways, considered to be at the core of the ryu, to animate it. They have been transmitted only to trusted members who have proven their loyalty and deep understanding of the ryu's curriculum.

Secret teachings? In flower arranging? Granted, the idea seems odd. It is, nevertheless, fundamental to ikebana. Some okuden are technical. The secrets are concerned with methods that will keep flowers fresh longer, or tricks that can be employed to bend stems without cracking or breaking them. Other okuden contain lessons the inner nature of which might not be revealed right away. The student of one ryu is taught that daffodils arranged as soon as they bloom in the spring are to be placed in the container with their blossoms bent down. If the student asks why, he or she might be told simply to be quiet and do it. That is the "kata." Only later, unless the student realizes it on his own, is the meaning behind the okuden given. Growing naturally at that time of year, daffodils would likely have been bent beneath a load of wet spring snow, and so the arrangement subtly reflects nature. Still other ikebana okuden involve specific combinations of plants or compositions which, like a fraternal handshake or password, serve as signs to other ryu initiates of the arranger's level of competency.

What is important about these okuden is that they demonstrate to some extent the depth of ikebana. The *kajin* or ikebana student, no more seeks to just make a pretty bouquet than the serious budoka is trying merely to learn self-defense. What appears on the surface is the form. What goes on underneath, invisible to all but those who have the sensitivity or who take the time to see it, is what is important. While making a pleasant arrangement of flowers, just as learning to fight or defend oneself in a violent encounter, are by-products of these studies, they are definitely not the aim. The goal of the budo and ikebana are goals consistent with all the Japanese *Do* forms. They are meant to be pursued as Ways of living. Self-discipline, the cultivation of moral energies, the creation of aesthetic form; these galvanize the spirit of ikebana just as surely and consistently as they do the arts of judo, kendo, aikido, and all the other Japanese budo. That is one reason ikebana is also known as and well deserves the appellation of *kado*, the Way of flowers.

The colors bloom and scatter. In this world, who lasts forever?

—Lotus Sutra

Okay, so your proposition is that there is nothing of great substance to distinguish between ikebana and budo, and that I may as well give up my kendo class and take up flower arranging, saving myself a lot of bruises and whacks? No. Put an ikebana master in a set of kendo *dogu* and out on the dojo floor, and he will be in a lot of pain. And I have known a number of highly ranked martial artists, none of whom, on the basis of their training alone, could explain to me the mechanics of a *shinputai* style of flower arranging. Yes, I know the famous story of the tea master who was required to face a swordsman. Fearing he would die because he'd never even held a sword before, he went to another expert swordsman and was given the advice to take a stance with the same spirit and concentration he would use in preparing tea. Next day at the duel, he does. His opponent is so unnerved by the composure of the tea master that he runs off. Good story. I asked my sensei about it once. He replied that it was, well, a good story. And added that in reality, the tea master would have, of course, died—but with a resigned equanimity. His corpse would have been composed. Spirit is a wonderful thing. It is not a substitute for technique.

The actual techniques of the Do are not the same. Learning to arrange flowers does not teach the mechanics of handling a sword. It would be preposterous to say that it does. What I am saying, however, is that ultimately, ikebana and the budo are two different approaches to climbing the same mountain. The methods are different. The training, in most ways, is not the same. The path taken will be of a different sort. Do not be fooled, however, by these distinctions. Both the kajin and the budoka, if their practice and study are correct, are trying to get to the same summit. And sometimes the differences in the apparently separate climbs of these two are not all that different at all.

Shussho, for instance, is a term used in ikebana. It refers to the most natural form of a flower or plant. It is shussho, or at least the representation of shussho, that the arranger attempts to re-create in his compositions. This is difficult. In fact, it is probably beyond the ability of all but a very few ikebana masters to do it deliberately and consistently. Consider trying to make an arrangement of iris that as perfectly as possible captures the true nature of that flower. What is the "perfect iris"? For most of us, even for most average ikebana practitioners, the approach would be to gather a dozen or so of these purple flowers and stand them upright in a container, trying to make them look as if they are growing naturally. But that is not really the shussho of the iris. The shussho is its most basic, elemental form. The Platonic ideal, in a way, of the iris. The more sensitive or talented among us might respond by taking only a single blossom and its stalk and presenting that as its shussho. But which one? There are, of course, no two irises alike and none are "perfect." This one might have a petal drooping. That one might have a crooked stem. When you look at it this way, the process of bringing out the shussho of an iris is extraordinarily challenging—impossible without years of training and no doubt a measure of innate talent.

The budo sensei has more than a passing familiarity with the notion of shussho. In the aikido dojo, for example, the teacher has a standard form by which a throw should be done. It is a model. He sets it, yet he cannot expect, nor does he desire that all his students will copy it slavishly and exactly. Criticisms that the traditional budo seek to create robotic clones of a "master" who despises and discourages any attempt at individuality are ignorant of what actually goes on in the dojo. The teacher sets the model, and the students try to copy it. But the intent here is not to produce a simulacrum of the sensei, although that might seem the case to the casual observer. The aikido sensei demonstrates *shiho-nage*. The students bow, pair off, and look as though they are trying to do it exactly as he has shown them. Some beginners may be trying to do just that. More advanced practitioners are trying to incorporate the *principles* of the throw as demonstrated. They are each different, in size or shape, from the sensei. They could not copy him precisely even if they tried. No, they are using his form to try to make their own shiho-nage work within the parameters he has set for them. After much practice, their own, unique shiho-nage will emerge, and that is the purpose of the lesson. (A note here: This unique interpretation of a technique or a kata does not happen quickly. The student adheres to the form, without any thought of his own version of it. Many years of complying with a standard ever so slowly becomes internalized to the extent that the individual's body type and personality will—if you'll forgive the pun— bloom. It flowers only after it has been watered and cultivated through hard training. I add this caveat as a warning for those students who will, when criticized by their sensei for their technique, reply that, "Well, it may not be 'right' by your standards, but it expresses my unique inner self." Un-unh. You have to *learn* the form and learn it deeply, before you can begin to merge into your own interpretation of it.)

The point is that the aikido sensei is trying to create an environment where the shussho of each of his students can develop fully. He does not want thirty copies of his throw. What he is striving for is that each will be unique, each an expression of the person doing it. It is a process every bit as difficult as arranging that iris to bring out the essence of the flower.

Interestingly, many of the same problems afflicting the budo today—abuse of power by teachers, petty political squabbling, the manipulation of the ranking system, and the failure of practitioners to comprehend the finer and more profound aspects of a Do—are exactly the same in ikebana organizations. If you ever have a chance to talk with a person doing ikebana, or the tea ceremony, you might be surprised to hear many of the same complaints you hear from your comrades in the dojo. This is understandable. The Do, as I said, might be different paths. But they are all going in a similar direction, and it is hardly surprising that the difficulties and frustrations encountered by one would be just as familiar to the others.

But what is the importance of flower arranging in the dojo? Kenji Nishitani, in his book *Kaze no Kokoro* (Shichosho, 1981), explains it very well. The flower of ikebana, he says, is "in the world of death, poised in death. It has become severed from the life which denies time and in doing so it has entered time and become momentary." While *ikebana* means literally "living blossoms," paradoxically, the materials used for flower arranging are not "living" at all. They are, as Nishitani notes, dead. They have been deliberately cut from their roots. Left alone in nature, their demise would scarcely have been noticed. Plants wither and die by the millions every day. A tree falls in the forest and whether it makes a sound or not is something for college sophomores to debate in dorm room bull sessions. But the fact is, they *do* fall, just as all plants do. As they droop, curl up, fade away in the garden outside, we are barely aware of the forsythia, the tulips, the apple blossoms dying. They pass from our world almost invisibly and usually slowly. Once they are cut, however, their death is highlighted, rendered imminent. It is the beauty of the masterful arrangement of ikebana we appreciate, certainly. Yet a more poignant sense of their beauty is found in the ephemerality that has, through their positioning in a container, been brought to our attention. This aspect of ikebana's beauty causes us to pause. We linger, appreciating, recognizing the impermanence it represents.

Nishitani's book makes the case for two approaches to art in general. There are those, he says, who attempt to deny temporality through their art. And there are those who celebrate it. Arts like sculpture and architecture are among the former. They are mediums that strive to step out of time and remain as enduring, to some degree. In contrast are those arts which, according to Nishitani, "enter into time." They accept the limitations of the moment. They exist and flower, but for a flicker of time. I am always reminded, thinking of the author's description, of a famous short story about a man who encountered Picasso while they were both walking on a beach. Picasso uses a stick to scribble a masterpiece in the sand. The man is transfixed by how wonderful it all is. And watches, heartbroken, as the tide comes in and washes it away. This celebration of transience is one Nishitani finds particularly conducive to Japanese forms of artistic expression. (It is worthwhile to note that even in those forms of Japanese art that might be categorized as stepping out of time and meant to be permanent, that there are cases—such as temple architecture where buildings are deliberately torn down and rebuilt periodically—that seem to fit more accurately into the ephemeral.)

The tea ceremony, Noh drama, haiku poetry; all of these last for an instant, or for the briefest span of time. They captivate us with their momentary beauty, offering a glimpse of their art form. Then they are done. Nishitani adds the art of flower arranging to this list of evanescent arts. I would suggest the budo should be added to it as well.

Do you karateka remember that beautiful, almost flaw-lessly executed rendition of the kata *Kanku-dai* you did last week? Everything seemed to come together. Your spirit and your body were working in a smooth and fluid coordination. Power was there at just the right moment, then relaxed. It may not have been perfect. But it was the best you know you can do. And of it, what remains? It existed for a few moments, then was gone, without leaving a single trace. Even if it had been filmed, the feeling, the intensity, the singularity of it all would not have been captured. You cannot replay it. You do not have to practice karate to understand this. Budo is about dealing with aggression. It is a form of combat. Whether the situations are rehearsed or confined to the realm of a sporting contest or for real, when an attack comes, there is little or no opportunity for contemplation or reflection. It simply materializes, and you must deal with it. In response—or if you are the attacker, in initiating it—your body flows, enters a stream of time. Tech-niques in the budo arise, take form, and then vanish. The mo-ment of the attack or the response cannot be recaptured. The technique cannot be "undone." There is a uniqueness of expe-rience in the budo that is as individual as the blooming of a morning glory in the summer—one that lasts not even as long as that flower's brief existence.

The phrase *ichigo; ichi-e,* or "one encounter; one chance," was used by Naosuke Ii in a treatise he wrote in the nineteenth century on the tea ceremony, *Chanoyu Ichi-e Shu.* Ii used ichigo; ichi-e to describe what he called the true spirit of the tea ceremony. The temporal quality of the art of tea, he said, "gives a feel of the exquisite evanescence of nature." The practice of budo demonstrates the same character. When people gather for a tea ceremony, there is inherent in the event the recognition that it cannot replicate any previous ceremony, nor can it ever be repeated. The host has but one chance to prepare tea for his guests in a beautiful way, with not a single clumsy or wasted motion. The guests have only this one opportunity to appreciate it. Whether they succeed or fail, the moment is gone. We do not think of it in this light, perhaps, but each time we step into the dojo, it is the same. We have only this time to make ourselves better than we were. Yesterday's efforts do not matter. Tomorrow's are a concern for tomorrow. What matters is right now. Ichigo; ichi-e.

Have you ever looked at a book of martial arts techniques and tried to follow the action from one photograph to the next? Have you ever watched a really skilled budoka doing a demonstration, trying to memorize just how it is he is moving? Most of us have. And we know how frustrating it is. Budo techniques have a spontaneity about them when they are done well that cannot be re-created. Trying to learn a kata from a book will always yield mechanical results at best. Imitate the expert's unrehearsed demonstration and it will inevitably look artificial. We who are serious about our training have all had to grapple with this aspect of the elusive nature of the arts. We have also been brought face-to-face with our own mortality when we train. A big part of the lessons of the dojo is that they can help to place us properly where we are in the scheme of things. It gives us a perspective on ourselves that is often missing in everyday life. We can easily come to believe that our accomplishments have some extraordinary significance. We have spent countless hours polishing our front kick and we can come to consider it remarkable. Our hip throws are the envy of the dojo. No matter how good we become, those flowers in the dojo are a constant reminder that these skills, too, are fleeting. The budo can do much to keep us young and supple and active, but they are not magic. We can surely live happier lives by following the martial Ways—but we cannot escape our own mortality.

Happy thoughts, huh? Gee, thanks. Maybe I will just skip practice this evening; stay home and wait for the Grim Reaper to make the call that's got to be coming sooner or later. No, no; the flowers that decorate the front of the training hall are not a symbol of gloom and despair. The idea of impermanence they represent, on the contrary, is just the opposite. *Mono no aware* is an aesthetic concept that goes quite far back in Japanese thought. Surely there are similar sentiments in other cultures, though I do not know of any that describe it so. *Mono no aware* is one of many phrases used to convey the thought that in a "recognition of life's impermanence," we come to develop an appreciation for how wonderful life is. Life's brevity is much of what makes it special. The last headmaster of the Urasenke ryu of the tea ceremony, Sen Soshitsu XV, was talking about the meaning of all Do forms being realized when they "excite us to do our best to realize each precious moment." In the budo, where with even the most conscientious of practitioners lies the constant possibility of injury or worse, there is a splendid opportunity to put into effect Soshitsu's words. Can't get motivated to go to the dojo tonight? Think for a moment that at any time, circumstances, illness, sudden responsibilities, or even your own death, might make it impossible to go in the future. You have the chance to train tonight, and to learn and to become a better person, for that is what motivates you to continue your study. So take it, knowing it will not always necessarily be there.

In *Kaze no Kokoro*, Nishitani explains what an arrangement of flowers does in a room:

The space of the entire room about them is drawn taut by the presence of flowers, as if it were charged with electricity. The air there is dynamic. While emanating a faint coolness from within and fathomless composure—like a person who has eradicated all attachments to life and abandoned all expectations fundamental to our mundane existence—through a complete silence they communicate that which is eternal.

Among "that which is eternal"—some of it anyway—are some changeless truths. We are not going to be around forever. The only way to *carpe diem* is to recognize that the day will pass, whether we make the effort to seize it or not, and so we may as well give every effort to make the most of it. From the greatest of events in our life to the most ordinary, these matter mostly in what we make of them. To come to the dojo is to recognize these truths. To arrange flowers and to display them at the front of the dojo is not only a tradition, not only a way of bringing some beauty into this place where we spend so much of our lives; it is also a powerful ritual in connecting with the timelessness of form, the fleeting nature of all the life that fills that form.

I read an interview of a karate sensei in Japan who was commenting on the attitudes of his best students. One, he noted, faithfully brought fresh flowers to the dojo each time she came. It was pleasant to hear of a student making such a gesture, more so to hear of a teacher who appreciated it. I hope other serious budoka will follow this example. Try it, if not regularly, at least once in a while. Come to the dojo early enough to have it to yourself, with flowers and a container. Unless you have had some experience in ikebana, your arrangement may not be all that great. No matter, at this point. Just a single blossom representative of the season, and a simple container to hold it with some water will do. And if there is no tokonoma at your dojo, surely there will be some other appropriate place. See how your arrangement makes you feel during the practice that follows. See how it makes the dojo feel to you. Perhaps it will do nothing. For sure, it isn't going to radically improve your technique or do anything miraculous like that. But you may gain some insight into words written over a thousand years ago in the collection of poetry, *Kokin-shu*:

> This much I have learned:
> The blossom that fades away, its color unseen
> Is the flower of the heart
> Of one who lives in this world.

13

Polishing the Mirror, Creating the Kata

Some years ago, a book on the Japanese martial arts came out, published in Europe and notable primarily for the wonderful color photographs it contained of many of Japan's ancient and modern fighting disciplines. It was a big, quarto-sized volume, a coffee-table book. It still appears sometimes in sales bins in bookstores. I imagine many of you have it. The text is minimal and, while adequate, it contains several errors. What interested me the first time I thumbed through this book, however, was a comment about the kata of Masatoshi Nakayama, the late chief instructor of the Japan Karate Association. Nakayama's favorite kata, according to the book, was *Meikyo*.

Meikyo, for those of you who do not know it, is an odd little karate kata. In the JKA and other of the larger Japanese karate organizations, it is not usually taught until one is quite far along. Only in a very few dojo is it regularly or seriously practiced. Meikyo is descended from one version of an Okinawan kata called *Rohai*. Matsumora Kosaku is supposed to have developed the kata in the mid-nineteenth century, based on some older sources, and so it is considered to be a kata of the Tomari lineage of the art. (Tomari, Shuri, and Naha are three towns, or, to be more exact, the first two are districts within the third, that spawned different versions of karate.) After Matsumora, the karate genius Itosu Yasutsune created three versions of Rohai. Gichin Funakoshi adapted the second of these when he brought his karate to mainland Japan in the first part of the twentieth century, and christened it with the name *Meikyo*, which means, "A Shimmering Mirror."

The name is, if you will forgive the pun, illuminating. Why did Funakoshi choose it? The original name, Rohai, refers to a "white heron." There are some one-legged stances in the kata that mimic the stance of a heron at rest, one leg tucked up. The meaning behind the stances has to do with pulling up a leg quickly in combat to avoid it being swept. Funakoshi's adaptation eliminated the one-legged stances, so perhaps he felt a name change was in order. There is a more likely explanation, however, if we know something of the character of Funakoshi. Gichin Funakoshi is one of the more extraordinary personalities of the martial arts scene of early modern Japan, a not inconsiderable achievement when you consider the company that includes. He was a product of both rural Okinawa and a privileged upbringing. His family was educated and, in terms of Okinawa, high-class. Still, in Japan he must always have been aware of his status as a bumpkin from a far-flung prefecture where, according to most Japanese, the people talked funny and had the manners of hillbillies. Almost from the moment he arrived in Japan, Funakoshi relentlessly worked to make himself acceptable to the Japanese and to integrate what was a native Okinawan folk art into the mainstream of the Japanese budo. The five *Pinan* kata used on Okinawa for training children in karate he renamed *Heian*, a nod to the great period of Japanese history. He substituted the name Meikyo for Rohai. It makes sense if you look at the opening movements of the kata, which resemble someone polishing a big mirror. I am betting Funakoshi, though, chose this name because he knew it would have a special significance to the Japanese he so wished to impress.

The first mirror, or meikyo, was, in Japanese mythology, one of the "three regalia," the sacred treasures of Shinto that are at the center of the story of Japan's creation. There was the sword, the one taken in battle with a giant serpent or crocodile or whatever it was (see chapter 11); and the *mitama*, or comma-shaped jewels. And the sacred mirror. The original is supposed to be housed in the inner precincts of a shrine in Ise. Copies of it are to be found (if you are allowed to look—and in most, only if you are a Shinto priest) in the innermost sanctuaries of most Shinto shrines all over Japan.

In Funakoshi's version of the kata, as I said, the performer makes a series of movements—double blocks—that resemble the polishing of a mirror. But the kata is also very rhythmic and dance-like, and that is the second connection Meikyo has with Shinto. To see where it started, we must go back into the mythology of that religion, to the creation of Japan itself.

Among the most powerful of the *kami*, the deities who ruled Japan during the mythic period, was Amaterasu, the "Heavenly-Shining-Deity." Her adventures, like those of all these ancient gods, are to be found in the *Kojiki* (the book of myths that we mentioned in chapter 11, when discussing the legendary origins of the schools of ninjutsu). Amaterasu was a female, but anyone foolish enough to think she was therefore weak and prissy would have been in trouble. She was the sort of female the National Organization for Women would adore. Once, for instance, when her brother took off, leaving Japan to go to Heaven, "causing the mountains and rivers to shake and every land and country to quake," Amaterasu suspected something was up. She twisted her hair into braids to get ready to fight, and on her back she slung a quiver filled with 1,500 arrows. She put armor on both arms designed to deflect arrows and took up a bow. According to the *Kojiki*, "she stamped her feet into the ground so strongly she sank up to her thighs in it, kicking away the earth like rotten snow."

Her brother, Susano-o—the same hero who fought the giant beast and took the sword from its tail—saw this. Without a pause, he said something equivalent to, "What, me? I'm not doin' nothin'." What followed was a verbal exchange, and from their words arose a mist that created many of the various lesser deities of Shinto. (This magical power imbued in words has had a profound effect on the martial arts, incidentally. The verbally expressed kiai, or combative shouts in classical schools of combat in Japan, can have esoteric connotations. Aikido's founder, Morihei Uyeshiba, is among many budoka who took an interest in *kotodama*, the role that sounds and words play in developing powers both physical and spiritual.)

Amaterasu was tough, no doubt about it. But she also had a petulant streak in her. And her brother was a divine pain in the neck. He broke dikes in the rice fields Amaterasu planted, and he "secretly voided excrement" in a sacred and purified hall where she was worshipping. Amaterasu had finally had enough. Probably it was the pooping-in-the-sacred-hall incident. Whatever, she retired in indignation to the "Rock Cave of Heaven." She was missed, too, since her seclusion meant the end of day and night, and as a result, the whole countryside was thrown into chaos. (As I mentioned in chapter 11, this may be more than just myth. It could have been a primitive memory of a minor ice age, or at least a series of very, very cold and dark years in prehistoric Japan when, geological evidence suggests, a series of severe volcanic eruptions could have caused clouds of ash to block out the sun.)

Several other kami convened to discuss the situation that was rapidly growing dire. They decided to try to talk or bribe Amaterasu out of the cave. One of the bribes they brought to the entrance of the cave was a mirror. (According to Shinto doctrine, it is this very same mirror which is still in a sacred hall at the shrine in Ise. All of Japan's emperors, including the present one, have gone to this hall, and they are the only ones who could tell us if the mirror is actually there.) The mirror, however, failed to do the trick. Nor did Amaterasu show any interest in any other of the gifts that were brought to her. She refused to leave the cave. In the end, it was up to another female kami, Ama no Uzume no Mikoto ("The Augustly Terrible Female of Heaven" is the best translation, and for those of you who might be expecting a girl, I think this is a name you ought to consider).

Ama no Uzume took a spear wrapped in long grasses and performed a dance in front of the cave. It was a dance so mesmerizing, so powerful, that Amaterasu was lured to the front of the cave to watch it. Once there, the other gods begged her to come home and to please, please get the sunshine going again. She agreed. (In case you're interested, the gods were rather irritated with her brother Susano-o for having caused this chaos in the first place. They fined him the equivalent of "one thousand tables" of offerings, and pulled out all his hair just for good measure.)

Partly because of such fascinating connections, I'd always taken a certain interest in the kata Meikyo. It was not among those taught me by my karate teachers from Okinawa. But when I began visiting regularly at a JKA dojo, I learned it. It contains a few movements that are difficult, including the *sankaku tobi,* or "triangular jump," that brings the karateka around 180 degrees, and a big, crescent-shaped kick unusual to karate. What is most challenging about Meikyo, though, is the rhythm. It is light and quick. But if you get in a hurry, you will miss the proper timing of the pauses that are important to its execution. I would practice Meikyo and wonder if my perform-ance was good enough to bring a deity out of her depression. And so, when I read in the book that it was the favorite kata of the JKA's chief instructor, I became even more interested in it. But the idea just didn't add up. Nothing I found in Japanese or English, interviews with Nakayama or his own writings, con-tained any special mention of Meikyo. It is, as I said, rarely practiced in the vast majority of JKA dojo. It seemed that if Meikyo was Nakayama's favorite, it would have been the sub-ject of a lot of enthusiasm. I was curious.

Finally, on a trip to Japan, I had the opportunity to ask some of the more senior members of the JKA about the quote from this book, about Nakayama sensei's purported fondness for Meikyo. Was the book correct? No, I was told, it was not. I spoke about it with a few of the senior instructors there, all of whom had known and trained under Nakayama for many years. They didn't know what I was talking about at first. But I finally concluded, based on what I was told, that the comment in the book was the result of a problem in translation. What Nakayama sensei may have actually told the author, one of the instructors said, was that he admired the spirit of kata as ex-pressed in Meikyo. Could you possibly explain this a bit fur-ther, I pressed. No, he said. You need to think about it. And so I have. And these are some of the conclusions I have reached:

Most often, when we enter into the practice of kata, we say that we are "doing" a kata, or that we "perform" it. Perhaps it might be better to think of the kata, however, as something that we create. Now this word will no doubt cause great consternation among the traditionalists out there, for whom it conjures up images of those poor deluded souls who fashion their own "forms," for the purpose of showing them off at tournaments, accompanied usually by bad and loud music. We do not need to create more kata in this sense. Hard as it may be for some of these sorts to believe, the curricula of karate kata is broad and deep enough. It will not measurably benefit from the contributions of some twenty-something-year-old "master" who decides to customize his own form. No, by *create*, I do not mean to say "make up." I am talking about a different process entirely.

When we begin to learn a kata, we are inevitably preoccupied with the mechanics of the movements. We are committing to memory certain sequences and getting them in the right order. Even in a short, relatively simple kata, that takes some time. After that task is accomplished, when we can go through the movements without having to stop and think about them, then we move on to the second stage of the kata learning process. We concern ourselves at the second stage with the correct application of speed, focus, force, and so on. This stage is even more difficult than the first. Conceivably, you could learn the outward movements of a kata by looking at photographs in a book and following along. But without a teacher to show you the rhythm and timing, the proper moment to be hard and focused and the times when you are supposed to be soft and fluid, you are lost. Every kata has its own "beat." Learning the motions of the kata is like learning to read the notes of a musical scale. The second stage, learning the beat, is how you begin to transform the notes into music.

The problem is that, for too many karateka, their approach to the kata culminates at this second stage. I have frequently encountered practitioners who have been working on one of the more advanced kata of karate—like one of the versions of Bassai or Kanku—for ten years or more, and they are still concerned with the various mechanics of the second stage. Such a concern is not unfounded, I hasten to add. We must always try to improve the basics of this second stage; polishing the combination of swift and slow, forceful and yielding, proper breathing and eye contact. Educating ourselves to read the notes and then to play the music is a crucial stage. We cannot stop there, however, if we want to perform at an advanced level. We have to go beyond mechanics and to interpret the music, to bring it alive. So too, the serious karateka must push on, into a third level of his approach to the kata, and that is when he should begin to create the kata each time he does it.

The kata do not exist as individual entities. We might say "Meikyo" in reference to a particular form. But Meikyo is not something out there running around like a horse or a dog. Meikyo, like all kata, comes alive, becomes a real thing, only when we enter into it, when we animate it. In this sense, we are creating the kata each time we do them. In this sense too, the kata are intensely, dramatically individualized in a way that those who have not encountered them at this level can hardly understand. Each "performance" of a kata, when engaged in at this third level, attains a quality of uniqueness. It becomes genuine.

Stepping out onto the dojo floor to participate in kata at this level has, in the consciousness of the karateka engaged in them, a feeling of incipience. We begin them the same way the potter sits down before a lump of clay. What will emerge from it? What form will it take? What expression will be generated from this moment of creativity? Each time we go through the kata, we have an opportunity—to create.

I think this may have been what Nakayama sensei had in mind when—or if—he said he admired the spirit of Meikyo. The kata allow us a chance to penetrate into the depths of karate—to see into its soul through the reflection of our own souls as we perform them. The name *meikyo* is a perfect reminder of that. Meikyo, as I mentioned previously, is best translated as "a shimmering mirror." A mirror was brought to the mouth of the cave as an inducement to draw out the goddess, along with the dance that eventually did the trick. Mirrors are to be found at the very center of many Shinto shrines today in Japan. As well, mirrors figure prominently in Buddhist imagery. A well-known Buddhist expression, "The Great All-Encompassing Mirror Wisdom," is a common reference to refer to the enlightened mind. Some karate masters have suggested that the proper attitude in going through the movements of Meikyo is one of "polishing" one's own mirror. I believe Nakayama's comments refer to Meikyo because of its name. But they could apply to all of the kata. We are, within them, capable of finding the way to polish our own mirrors, mirrors that reflect inward, to our innermost selves.

I have, perhaps, written here more about Meikyo, that odd and seldom-practiced little kata, than anyone else has, in English or in Japanese. Perhaps I have made too much of what, after all, began as a possible conjecture resulting from a probable mistranslation in a book. Yet I suspect that within the mirror of Meikyo—as within all of the kata—we can find something of substance and value reflected back. With that metaphor in mind, I would like to close this discussion with a poem that, while written not by a martial artist but by the fifteenth-century Noh master, Zenchiku Ujinobu, nonetheless hints at the meaning of the mirror in karate's kata:

Dave Lowry

Masu kagami	The clear mirror—
ura wo katachi no	Know that which lies behind it
omote nite	by means of its reflected forms
omote wo ura no	as well as by that appearing on its face
hikari to mo shire	by knowing of the light that lies behind it.

14

Classical Japanese Martial Arts in the West

Problems in Transmission

It is, almost undeniably, a fundamental aspect of the American character to be more or less constantly in search of something better. We seem to have almost a genetically predisposed desire for something different, something out of the ordinary. We are, to put it less charitably, perhaps, easily bored. In a more idealistic light, we acknowledge that such a cultural restlessness sparked our Manifest Destiny, beginning with the arrival of the Puritans to Massachusetts Bay and, most recently, with men walking on the moon. Ours is an approach to life that has influenced the behavior of Americans in matters as great as the way in which we started and continue to build a nation, or as trivial as our search for the next, best microbrewery. Somewhere in the middle there is the way we have sought out martial disciplines of Japan that have interested us over the years. As it has been with so many other searches, the grass, putting it simply, has always been greener on the other side of the hill.

In the case of those martial arts in this country, if we trace their presence here back far enough, we can see that the problem has been that there just weren't all that many hills, green or otherwise, around. In the fifties, judo was utterly exotic. Outside of some Japanese-American enclaves, it was little known and less practiced and taught. And even in such ethnic communities, karate was so rare that when it was publicly demonstrated in Hawaii in 1927, the event occasioned an article in a Honolulu newspaper. Within a decade, that changed. In the sixties, karate became commonplace. By the latter half of that decade, most cities had several dojo, or "studios" or YMCAs, that were offering instruction in the art. In the seventies, the green meadows available for grazing in the martial arts became even more numerous and varied. Kung-fu was added, as were several other combative arts from various parts of Asia. Most of them were more attractive (because they were "newer," and thus, more exotic, primarily) alternatives to the karate and judo that had become, by then, pedestrian. To meet the grazing appetites of the interested public, there was also no shortage of arts that were more or less concocted, e.g., ninjutsu, created out of folklore or ambitious fictions. In the eighties and nineties, this continued, and martial arts enthusiasts found themselves with a smorgasbord of sorts, including *silat, muay Thai, sambo,* and a host of other disciplines.

In light of all this searching for something new, not to mention the entrepreneurial instincts to feed the search, it should hardly be surprising that the turn of the twenty-first century has found attention being directed at still another fertile field of combative arts. The first few years of this century have seen a new pasture open up in the form of the *bujutsu,* the classical martial skills of the feudal period in Japan, *circa* 1400–1867.

The bujutsu, also referred to as the koryu (literally, it means the "old" or "ancient traditions") offer a lot of attractions to the enthusiast in search of pastures more lush. Among the obvious reasons why Westerners in the twenty-first century might be drawn to arts that were meant for Japanese of the warrior class centuries ago would be:

Venerability. Despite our twenty-first century appetite for all that is new or faddish, a sizable number of us have a respect for the merits of age. Anything as ancient as the koryu, the reasoning follows, must have some value.

Romanticism. Popular novels and movies have glamorized "samurai swordsmanship" to levels best described as swashbuckling. The samurai himself—a warrior who dressed in fine silks and pursued poetry and the tea ceremony, who made a life of blood and beauty—these are images that are tremendously appealing to many people. Look at the popularity of groups that "re-create" medieval culture and stage mock battles and jousts and such. Add the supposed mysticism of "The Far East," and you can see where arts like the bujutsu would fascinate so. A lack of reliable information placing these arts in a realistic historical context has left a gap that romantics have been free to fill in with their own notions of chivalry, derring-do, and so on.

Elitism. The rarity of the koryu provides an attraction for many of those individuals who enjoy standing out from the crowd, or at least who appreciate not following along with it. There may be three or four "karate black belts" on the average block in most cities in the U.S. But how many "master swordsmen" or "modern samurai" are there?

Efficacy. Since these arts have a battlefield provenance, there is the assumption that the koryu contain many secrets, particularly lethal techniques that make them more effective in modern civilian self-defense situations.

Integrity. Anyone even tangentially involved with the average budo organization devoted to aikido, judo, karate, or some other martial Way, has been exposed to mendacity, avarice, and managerial incompetence on a truly grandiose level. The koryu are (incorrectly) perceived as being above the organizational squabbles, the preoccupation with ranks, and the endless quest for more power and money that appear to compromise and infect the philosophy and goals of the modern and popular budo forms.

These, generally, are the views Western enthusiasts who are well-read (and books are almost the only remotely reliable source from which they might gather information, since non-Japanese with advanced experience in the koryu are so rare) have of the classical bujutsu. Very briefly, the koryu bujutsu might be more objectively defined as those combative forms directly or indirectly of a battlefield nature, that were the exclusive domain of the professional man-at-arms in pre-modern Japan. They date, as noted above, from approximately the fifteenth to seventeenth centuries. They are distinguished from the more familiar twentieth-century budo forms in several ways.

An important note here: My use of "bujutsu" and "budo" to contrast ancient and modern combative arts in Japan is one first suggested by the late Donn Draeger. Draeger pioneered much if not most of the study of the Japanese martial disciplines in the West. He needed a way to highlight the distinctions between the classical arts of the samurai and the martially oriented arts and sports that developed after the end of the feudal period. He chose the bujutsu/budo taxonomy. It is far from perfect for explaining the distinctions. There are numerous koryu with undeniably ancient roots that refer to their arts as "budo," for example. In everyday Japanese, the two terms can be used interchangeably, and they often are. If you tell the average

Japanese that you do a "bujutsu," he is apt to think you have somehow learned an odd and somewhat dated word to describe budo. Even if you explain the difference, it will probably not be clear to him; most Japanese don't know anything about the feudal-era arts, and assume that their samurai forebears were, three hundred years or so ago, doing kendo or judo.

Draeger's arbitrary use of budo and bujutsu has been criticized by some younger generations of martial arts enthusiasts. Some of them have serious points to make. Most of them hope their dialectical potshots will enhance their status by "taking on" a respected authority like Draeger. I trust the reader will bear in mind that I am using these terms as Draeger did, because they serve to contrast significant differences in classical and modern approaches to martial disciplines, and because I (like all his critics) cannot think of a more suitable terminology.

That said, here are four of the most obvious characteristics that distinguish the older traditions from the modern arts:

The bujutsu are:

- intended for implementation by a professional (feudal-era) military class rather than for a general population.

- far less influenced by Zen Buddhism than later forms of budo. The spiritual underpinnings of the koryu tend to be those of *mikkyo*, a form of esoteric Buddhism.

- invariably and without exception organized under the aegis of the ryu, a feudal institution of old Japan with pedagogical, political, and cultural aspects that are completely different from modern commercial enterprises.

- obviously completely bereft of a sporting element, contests, or the dan-i ranking systems (usually signified with colored belts) that are central to budo forms.

Undeniably, the koryu are appealing to a Western audience. At the risk of drawing out my analogy about greener pastures too far, however, those audiences would do well to remember that the color of a meadow may not be a positive indication that the grass there is palatable, that it is nutritious, or that it is even healthy for those who want to consume it. Several Westerners have gone to Japan to investigate the koryu. Some have gained admission to these classical ryu. A few have pursued them at such an intense and protracted level that they have attained a thorough understanding of these arts. A very few have been granted permission to teach either part or all the curriculum of the ryu to which they belong. (As we shall see, this permission is absolutely crucial if the ryu is to remain viable; one never undertakes to teach a koryu without the explicit permission, often in writing, of a qualified teacher.)

Nearly all of these individuals followed the trail blazed in the mid-sixties in Japan by the late Donn Draeger, introduced above. Draeger, a former Marine officer, took a scholarly and a participatory interest in the martial Ways that were being practiced in postwar Japan. His activity eventually led him into the koryu. Not only did Draeger's expertise impress several Japanese koryu experts enough for them to allow other foreigners to enter their ryu, he enthusiastically supported the education of many young foreign adepts living and training in Japan during the sixties and seventies.

We must remember, not incidentally, that the numbers of Western koryu participants about which we're speaking here were at that time (and still are) minuscule compared to the thousands of foreigners studying the modern budo in Japan. A generous estimate of the non-Japanese who have had serious instruction in the koryu would be no more than a few dozen. Their interests and experiences tend to create a certain cliquishness. They know or know of one another in a way completely unfamiliar to the large and largely anonymous groups involved in the budo. This is important to consider, since those koryu exponents claiming to be legitimate but who are unknown to this fraternity of practitioners are apt to be regarded by the latter with considerable suspicion.

In contrast to this group of foreign practitioners of koryu are those persons interested in these arts who have attempted to involve themselves in the bujutsu in different ways. There is no shortage of such people. There are, in fact, enough of them to create quite a market for the classical martial arts, and as with any appetite, there have been those who are eager to satisfy, to present a product. As a result, there are many individuals in the West who have been led to believe they are learning the skills of this koryu or that. They are, more accurately, being misled into believing. Fraud and deception involving the classical bujutsu have become a sad and reprehensible aspect of the martial arts scene in this country. Not so despicable but equally regrettable has been the amount of confusion and misinformation that has characterized Western perceptions of these martial traditions.

The problems encountered by the would-be *bugeisha*, the practitioner of the bujutsu, are varied. At one end of the scale are those students learning a legitimate system of feudal-era combat, but who are doing so under a "teacher" who does not have the permission of a teacher before him that grants him license to transmit the system. (Also found at this range of the spectrum is at least one case where a teacher has actually been given official permission to teach more for political or sentimental reasons than for technical proficiency, and who is simply incompetent as an instructor.) At the other extreme are charlatans who have actually created their own systems, passing them off with faked lineages and other false provenances. All these problems share a common source. All may be traced back to some fundamental misunderstandings about the nature of the bujutsu and the koryu that have sustained and nurtured them.

The ryu itself is something of a mystery to the modern world. It is a wholly feudalistic institution with a fascinating history. As with any organized combat, the kind of hardship in battle faced by the samurai in old Japan required a virtually inviolable cohesion between individual warriors in order to create an effective, functioning unit. In no small part, the martial ryu served to establish this connection. Loyalty, identification with the group, a willingness to place the goals of that group above one's own goals (specifically the goal of self-preservation)—these qualities were as crucial to the maintenance and survival of a combative ryu as was the transmission of technical skill. Consequently, the ryu can be understood in terms of being a "family" as much as it was a school or a distinctive tradition.

It was and is quite different from a modern commercial budo dojo, in at least three important ways:

One: In the koryu there are no "champions." The karate school may feature one or two stars who shine at the competitions and who often use others in their school as little more than sparring partners. But the koryu is, on the proving grounds of the battlefield, only as strong as the weakest link in its membership. There is a sense of responsibility among members, then, for everyone's development.

In this sense, the koryu are not nearly so egocentric as are the modern budo. If today's budo dojo really wanted to do things "the samurai way" as they often imagine or advertise, they could begin in this fashion: at the next tournament, every competitor representing the school should give up his trophies unless the majority of his dojo-mates have won their matches as well. After all, on the battlefield, where the real samurai way was in effect, individual accomplishment is relatively meaningless unless the whole group succeeds.

Secondly, the ryu depends upon a pedagogical method very different from the way judo, aikido, and karate are taught today. The modern budo exponent follows a standardized form in his training. He is forced to make numerous concessions to learning in a large class. With forty or fifty students, it may be months before the student of karate or aikido, for instance, can expect any individual attention from the teacher. (One well-known aikido instructor in this country has clearly explained in interviews that not all the people practicing at his dojo are his students. Only after they have persevered in their training sufficiently to have advanced to a particular degree of skill does he consider them actually "his.")

The koryu exponent follows a set form as well in his training, learning kata or techniques in a loosely prescribed order. But his teacher, by the very nature of the ryu, confines his teaching to within a small group. From the beginning of his learning, the koryu student receives very individualized tuition. An epigram of the koryu explains it this way: "Ten different students; ten different arts." The teaching, to some extent, adapts to the student.

Sometimes, in those koryu that have curriculum involving more than a single weapon in their arsenal, one student may begin learning one weapon while another beginning at the same time will be taught to use another one. This virtually private instruction means that the koryu sensei can take into account differences in the physique, temperament, and background of his students and can teach them accordingly. All will, if they continue their practice, end up learning the same curriculum. They won't learn it, however, at the same time or in the same way. This individualized teaching is nearly impossible in a budo dojo with dozens and dozens of members who must, logistically, be taught all the same.

Thirdly—and most importantly—the individual koryu exists as a distinct social group. It is, as noted above, much like a family. This implies a limited availability to outsiders, much as your own family has a limited flexibility, if it is to remain a distinct family unit, for accepting outsiders.

Consider this: Aside from being born or adopted into it, one enters your family only through marriage. Think about how protracted this latter process is. How long does it take before your spouse or brother- or sister-in-law is fully integrated into your family? How long before they learn all the family nicknames, family stories; learn which cabinets hold the dishes at your house, or how to best handle Uncle Harry when he gets drunk and starts telling off-color tales about his wartime visits to brothels in Manila? It is a long process, one that cannot be hurried. There are no shortcuts to being absorbed by a family, becoming a part of a small group like that. And most of us have had the experiences, in our own families, of those who try to enter but just can't. Because of their personality or because of the nature of the family itself, some outsiders never do entirely fit in. You can't have a seminar to teach these people what they need to know, how they need to behave to be accepted. You cannot force someone to fit into your family if they do not.

This analogy is entirely apt in describing the typical koryu. Their structure makes them unsuitable for access to large numbers of outsiders. There was a movie some years ago; perhaps you have seen it on cable or video, titled *The Challenge*. It starred

Toshiro Mifune, and it contained scenes of group training at what was supposed to be a koryu school. Pairs of practice partners in the movie neatly lined up and simultaneously went through choreographed movements. I was amused to see that a little more than twenty years later, scenes in the movie *The Last Samurai* depicted martial training exactly the same way. This may be the way those who have never visited one might believe a koryu group is run. But to those who have visited or trained in a real koryu, these scenes rang particularly false. Mass instruction has never been a feature of these arts, and cannot be. It takes years to instruct and impart all the technique and lore and history of a koryu to a single student. It is a considerable investment in time. Learning a koryu resembles more a master-apprentice relationship than it does a situation with the teacher-at-the-head-of-the-class model for education that we have become accustomed to in modern times. It is as well an extremely close relationship, and the personality of the sensei will, without a doubt, profoundly affect the character of his students. This is a relationship that can only develop properly by a near-daily interaction between teacher and student, in training and in other activities.

Once a person has this basic knowledge of the family nature of a legitimate koryu, and can see how its individualized instruction further limits participation, he can see how long and how close the process is to inculcate a person into the ryu. Consequently, the methods typifying the fake koryu will seem quite inappropriate, to say the least. Can you understand the derision that meets announcements of "seminars" open to all who pay their fees, that propose to teach a classical martial art?

The whole subject of commercialism in the koryu is another one that is difficult for us to grasp in the twenty-first century, with our mercantile-based societies. When it comes up, those who claim to be teaching a classical system in return for the remuneration found in a commercial-type school invariably point to a single episode in the history of the martial arts to justify their actions. They cite the case of Uyeshiba Morihei, aikido's founder, who paid a specific sum for specific techniques taught him by his occasional mentor, Takeda Sokaku, a teacher of the Daito-ryu. This is a non sequitur because: a) Uyeshiba was not even born until after the end of Japan's feudal period; he was a modern martial artist, not a classical one; b) the Daito-ryu does not meet the standards of a koryu in the strictest parlance; and c) Takeda Sokaku can hardly be considered a typical teacher in the koryu tradition.

Historically, payment for instruction in a koryu was largely moot. The ryu would have been financially maintained by a clan or a daimyo (warlord/clan leader) to which its headmaster belonged. The headmaster may have had other, administrative duties to perform in addition to his responsibilities for teaching the martial arts. Other bujutsu masters were retained under the auspices of a Buddhist temple that served as the spiritual home of that particular ryu. Today, almost no one in Japan makes a living teaching a legitimate koryu. It is an avocation. Training fees or dojo dues are minimal. They are usually used for the upkeep of the training facilities. Anyone claiming to be teaching a classical bujutsu who is charging exorbitant fees ought to be subject to the most careful scrutiny. Of the roughly half dozen authorities I know of who are instructing some sort of koryu system in the U.S., none is charging for their teaching or making a profit on the arrangement.

Another aspect of the historical koryu that causes misunderstanding concerns their place in Japanese society. More than one ersatz "classical martial arts ryu" being sold in this country attempts to explain its lineage as a *sub-rosa* system that escaped the attention, deliberately or inadvertently, of researchers who have extensively cataloged Japanese martial ryu, both extant and extinct. Not long ago, I was sent a hugely entertaining collection of letters between a bujutsu researcher in Japan and a senior student of a supposed koryu practiced exclusively here in the United States. The researcher was inquiring about the history of the ryu. The senior student had all kinds of the most outrageous explanations for this ryu's having failed to catch the attention of every serious martial arts researcher in the world. The ryu's lineage had been left out of this or that book by accident, he first said. The headmasters of the ryu were forced into living anonymously after the Second World War as the result of anti-martial arts policies during the Occupation, was a later claim. It went on and on, and the researcher calmly and logically refuted each of these tales.

True, he said, the books did leave out some ryu accidentally. But it is unlikely that every dictionary of Japanese koryu would leave out the same ryu by making the same error. And why weren't other koryu masters forced to live underground and conceal their ryu? The exchange finally ended when the senior student was driven to suggest that all history is subjective, and that none of the histories of the various koryu are at all dependable for scholarship. Such a position is quite close, intellectually, to those who insist the Holocaust never happened; one hardly knows whether to continue to try to reason with them, or merely pity them in their sad delusions.

The "secret ryu" is a convenient story in explaining away any lack of outside historical documentation or a provenance that can be independently verified. But the truth is, it's a story that, in terms of the koryu, doesn't have much credibility. Remember this one fact: The martial ryu in feudal Japan was a political unit. The ryu existed to further the interests of a clan or a daimyo. An underground ryu would have been as viable and as effective as an underground political party in a democracy. Can you imagine trying to persuade voters to support your platform, but concealing from them at the same time the fact that your party exists? No. Sooner or later, for the party to be effective, its presence must be made known. A ryu was not much different during the feudal era (although of course, today it may be: very few Japanese are even aware of the koryu). Certainly all bujutsu ryu had their secrets. But secret ryu? Not in Japan.

If not exactly secret, other impostors claim, their ryu are simply so obscure they have been overlooked by numerous and expert martial arts researchers and historians. This is an interesting claim—not because it's true; almost invariably, it is not—but because it reveals how one culture (ours, in this case) can unknowingly transpose its own history and social customs on another (in this instance, that of Japan).

America is a large country. A very large one. It has always been a country that allowed, in comparison with the rest of the world, an equally enormous freedom in the personal lives of its citizens. Daniel Boone didn't have to consult with any authority or government agency when he left Pennsylvania to go to the far frontier of Kentucky. He took off the same way you might take off to go on a holiday this weekend. Neither you nor he had to get permission for travel, or tell authorities where you were going or when you might return.

Boone didn't have to fill out any documents or carry any official papers with him. Record keeping of such movements are, to the frustration of many a genealogist, scarce. If I told you my ancestors began a pottery tradition 230 years ago in northern Georgia, and I am doing the same kind of pottery today in my home in Oregon, you would have little evidence to dispute my story, should you choose to do so. How would you do it? You might ask if there was any mention of my ancestors' occupation as potters back in colonial Georgia in old census records. But I could say, nope; they lived way back in the woods of Appalachia where census takers never made it. They never were required to register their trade, nor did they have to have any documentation of their eventual migration to Oregon.

In short, my story is perfectly believable in the context of American history and culture. A Japanese claiming a similar kind of artistic past, however, could not falsely do so any longer than it would take an interested party to check voluminous and extensive records that are easily and publicly available in Japan.

Japan is a small country. It has almost always been sedentary in terms of population. And because of the control of the daimyo over virtually the entire country, there were records kept on nearly every person in the domains of those leaders. It would likely be possible, if I were a Japanese with ancestral roots in the art of pottery, to establish the nature of my predecessors' ceramics inventory in any given year, to discover exactly where their kilns were located, and certainly, to learn if they had relocated to another part of the country; these would in most cases be easy facts to uncover. There would be notations of these in provincial and local records.

This is much the same situation as can be found among martial arts practitioners in Japan. The information available to martial arts researchers and scholars is staggering. If there is any problem in reconstructing the histories of the various koryu, it is often that there is too much information. It requires some patience to sift through it all. With a little digging, it is possible to discover not just the basic facts about the thousands of koryu that have existed, but their lineages, complete or nearly so, as well as all sorts of quotidian details about the lives and activities of past masters. It is possible that a koryu could have slipped through such a tight and far-flung net of information. But if a potential student of such a tradition is considering joining it as it is taught in this country, he must be willing to bet on two remarkably unlikely occurrences. He must believe that such a ryu has passed undetected through that tight web of historical scrutiny and research. He must also believe that an American was able to enter and to master such an obscure system and now professes legitimately to teach a ryu that the Japanese have never heard of.

I don't want to overstate the situation here. It *is* possible for an art to have thrived in obscurity, growing in such deep shadows that all the other practitioners of related arts remain unaware of its existence. And records in Japan have been subject to a world war that destroyed all kinds of documents. But let us summarize the whole subject of secret or rare koryu allegedly being taught in this country. The tales surrounding these systems are undeniably appealing. They evoke romantic and exciting scenes of a mountain fastness populated by wizened masters of mayhem, passing deep and deadly secrets along to loyal acolytes. Look, though, at the historical facts. A daimyo ruled his lands through taxation of his subjects. He worried constantly about insurrections or clandestine political foment. Does it seem plausible he would be unaware of a clan of those hidden masters living on his property, his land, without paying taxes? Would he allow them to be secretly practicing and promoting a fighting art that could, in all likelihood, be used against his own samurai if he permitted it to continue?

Daimyo usually ascended to power, and they almost always remained there, by controlling things. The roads, the waterways, the people under their rule. And it's not as though there was a vast frontier where their authority did not extend. Punishments were strict and harsh for even the mildest threats to their rule. I don't know about you, but I'd have some serious questions about any stories of a secret martial ryu that could have survived under those conditions.

The way in which a koryu is maintained and passed on is still another source of misunderstanding for the Western enthusiast of the classical Japanese martial disciplines. The bujutsu of Japan share an internal structure almost identical to those of ryu devoted to the art of flower arranging (ikebana), the tea ceremony (chado), and other arts of the feudal period. The structure is called the *iemoto* system.

Have you ever thought about who actually "owns" a martial art? There are copyright laws that enjoin you from using the title Shito Ryu Itosu Kai, true. But you cannot be punished through our legal system by teaching all the kata and other methods of that organization, even if you learned them by watching some videos and never had the blessing of the Itosu-kai at all. The same is true for various schools of aikido, or any of the Japanese budo.

A classical martial ryu, though, was actually owned, in a sense. It was the property, literally, of its originator, or of his descendants. The founder, or iemoto, designated his successor, who became the next headmaster or owner of the system. The line of succession was usually a familial one, father to eldest son. On occasion, adoption might have been necessary to carry on the lineage. Other ryu were passed down to a trusted disciple outside the family. The salient point for our purposes of understanding this iemoto system is that the responsibility, the privilege of teaching or transmitting a koryu, was and still is rather tightly controlled. It is entirely different from a modern budo like karate-do, where anyone at any time is free to begin teaching.

Different koryu that still exist today take different approaches to the whole matter of who is allowed to teach them. In most, a certification of mastery is not necessarily a license in itself to teach. To actually oversee instruction, one must usually seek the specific permission (or be granted it) from the incumbent headmaster. In others, the designation of mastery is an official declaration that the holder is de facto allowed to provide instruction in the ryu. In some cases, those who have mastered the ryu will be granted a limited permission to teach certain aspects of the curriculum, with the understanding that the students of the teacher will eventually take more advanced instruction under the headmaster or some other designated senior. (This is precisely the case with an exponent of one koryu that is currently being taught in the U.S. The "teacher" was leaving Japan to pursue a business opportunity. He lacked advanced instruction in the ryu, although he wanted to continue his training. The headmaster of the ryu gave him informal permission to teach some rudiments of the art to a limited number of students. But it is important to recognize that such instruction cannot be considered the equivalent of membership in that ryu, nor should those receiving this teaching hold any misconceptions about their status within the system.)

The aspiring koryu practitioner should make every effort to learn how the teaching hierarchy in a particular koryu is maintained before he begins an association with it. This is vital if the teaching presented is being done so outside of Japan. If he is satisfied that he comprehends the criteria for teaching and he believes his prospective teacher meets it, he should feel confident in pursuing the art under such tutelage.

A good example here is found in the Katori Shinto-ryu. The oldest of the martial koryu still practiced in Japan, the Shinto-ryu's present iemoto is Iizasa Yasusada, a twentieth-generation descendant of the ryu's founder, Iizasa Choisai Ienao. A congenital health condition prevents the current headmaster from teaching in the ryu. That responsibility has fallen to the ryu's designated chief instructor, Otake Risuke, who teaches at his dojo in Narita. Most readers will know this. There are, however, at least three other people currently teaching the curriculum of the Shinto-ryu. These three teachers have varying degrees of expertise in the art. Certainly, all of them can prove that they studied the Shinto-ryu. None of these three, though, can or does claim that they have the sanction of the headmaster to do what they are doing.

For some aspiring practitioners, the experience of these three may be sufficient. They all have students here in the U.S. Other would-be practitioners, however, may decline to practice any form of the Shinto-ryu unless they can be accepted by that ryu's primary lineage. But all of them should be cognizant of the facts and make their decisions accordingly.

It is a cognizance of facts that is most crucial for the prospective student of any koryu. He needs the facts to take the opportunity (and it is an extremely rare one) to begin a study of a koryu that may be available in the West. More likely, he needs facts to steer him clear of fraudulent ryu, or from those teachers who may sincerely believe they are imparting an authentic classical system of combat strategy when they are not. Most importantly, knowing the facts surrounding the bujutsu is the best way to see these wonderful old arts not as others would romantically like them to be, but as they actually are.

One reason that fraudulent koryu and ersatz "masters" have proliferated in the West is a rather (at the risk of sounding sexist) gentlemanly refusal to speak or write critically of others in public on the part of legitimate koryu members and authorities. There has also been an attitude of "anyone foolish enough to become involved in a phony koryu deserves what he gets." Doubtless, some reluctance to speak out stems from a stubborn, almost religious fervor with which adherents to these false koryu support and defend them.

My own experience in dealing with these individuals has been illustrative. As it was with the correspondence I mentioned above, between a researcher in Japan and a senior student of a fake master in the United States, in the face of overwhelmingly objective evidence that shows them that the system they are studying has no historical reality, their response, pathetically, is often, "My teacher says it's so." At this point, the researcher must conclude he is dealing with a person caught up with a belief system. Facts are not so important to these people as are images, both of themselves and their teachers, that affirm a particular view of things.

Fortunately, not all individuals training in a fake koryu are so dogmatic. Some, through their own efforts or by approaching authorities with their questions, come to discover they are being misled and cheated. One courageous and refreshingly honest confession appeared not long ago in a martial arts publication. The writer admitted that he had fallen in with a dishonest instructor of a bogus koryu, and that he had contributed to this problem by creating kata and other aspects of training on his own.

Unlike others who cling to their phony ryu, this fellow, according to his writing, came to see that he would never attain the goals that brought him to a search for the bujutsu in the first place if he continued. In my opinion, this person has taken an enormous step forward in his approach to the classical martial arts, and toward his own self-mastery.

The intent of writing this is not to ridicule or to unfairly cast aspersions. If the reader has an opportunity to pursue a true and authentic koryu in this country and he is so motivated, then he should by all means do so. (As you must now realize, this is an extremely unlikely proposition for most. I noted earlier that I can think of only a half dozen real koryu experts in the U.S. They all keep a low profile. Some currently have no students at all; others have no more than three or four. None—and this is a crucial point—none of them is in the least bit evasive about their training history or qualifications if they are asked. Each can give you the addresses of their teachers and the dojo where they trained in Japan, and can provide documentation and genealogies that can easily be verified in that country.)

The classical martial disciplines of Japan are a rich source of physical, spiritual, and social value. They are a treasure every bit as precious as any work of art. If the prospective practitioner should not be hasty to jump into a ryu of questionable legitimacy, neither should he adopt an attitude of cynicism that leads him to overlook a chance to join a koryu. (I am reminded of perhaps the senior-most koryu authority outside Japan, a scholar, author, and true master, who oversees a small group of trainees in his art in Hawaii. It has occurred more than once that a spectator at outdoor training sessions will inquire about joining, only to lose interest when it is explained that the master is of Caucasian rather than Japanese ancestry.)

To return, if I may, in summation, to the analogy of the "greener pastures." The bujutsu are a lush meadow for all those willing and able to enter them. Those who cannot make this entrance can show a real appreciation and respect for these arts by refusing to compromise them, by refusing to accept a cheap imitation. If they are a landscape that can only be viewed from a distance, those who truly admire the bujutsu in the West will show the nature of their character by doing just that.

15

Confessions of a Navy SEAL

I made a confession recently to my dojo-mates. It is a secret I've kept for a long time and I wanted to share it with them. At morning practice, I confessed:

I am a Navy SEAL.

"You weren't even in the military," one of them said.

"You told me the only time you ever even had on a scuba tank was in the shallow end of an apartment building swimming pool, and you nearly passed out 'cause you couldn't figure out how to use the regulator," said another.

"If you're a SEAL, show us your enlistment papers, some kind of proof," said another. "Introduce us to some members of your team."

Unbelievers. That fluff is merely window dressing. I tried to explain. I am a Navy SEAL because I have always wanted to be one. I feel like one. I conduct myself like one. I even have a mentor who's taught me what he says SEALs learn, and he's very happy with my training. What more proof do you need?

I'm thinking about leaving these guys and finding a dojo more amenable to my way of thinking. If mail I've gotten from time to time over the years is any indication, there are plenty of them out there. Places where my status as a Navy SEAL would not be questioned and would be properly respected. A lot of this mail came as a result of an article I wrote for the Journal, *Furyu* (reprinted here as chapter 14). I was trying to explain the problems faced by Westerners wishing to train in a classical martial koryu. I outlined the nature of the koryu and mentioned the growing number of frauds that have emerged. I mentioned alleged ryu concocted entirely by self-appointed masters and others that are pale and mistaken imitations of the real systems. I pointed out some of the glaring discrepancies of those who are pretending to teach them. And I made some suggestions for those who wish to experience legitimate koryu, difficult as they are to find in this country.

In response, I heard from some readers who took exception to my arguments and explanations. Their responses may be summed up roughly as follows:

1. There is no clear-cut, exact definition of a classical koryu. Therefore, any one that comes along may be so labeled, and those of us who take exception are snobs.

2. Practical skills are the only true and objective criteria of one's claims about associations or memberships in a koryu, and these ought to take precedence over papers, licenses, or other documentation. If one looks like an exponent of a koryu, behaves that way, and demonstrates abilities we might expect from a practitioner of a koryu, they should be so considered and respected. No one owes anyone an explanation or documentation of their claims regarding membership in a koryu. It is boorish to inquire.

3. If one feels good about his practice, is sincere, and trains with an "open heart"—if one meets the expectations of one's teacher—that is all that is necessary.

4. No one in the West is really doing a koryu because a) we aren't ethnically Japanese, b) there is no practical implementation of these arts on the battlefield, and c) all of them have been changed or altered with the passing of time, and so claims of authenticity are meaningless and more an attempt to "say what we are a part of" than to establish a legitimate lineage.

It is interesting to note that such arguments, especially the last one, are relatively recent in origin. It is even more cogent that these arguments—again, especially the last one—come in large measure from exponents of questionable arts who, only a few short years ago, were vociferous in their protestations that their ryu were historically sound and a product of feudal Japan. They wrote detailed accounts of their rituals, training, and curriculum, replete with lineage charts. Alas, more and more good scholarship about the martial koryu is being produced in English. It is becoming progressively harder to present claims that one's art is "four hundred years old," or that one is the inheriting headmaster of a ryu that has coincidentally escaped the scrutiny of generations of scholars and researchers.

With more being authoritatively written about the true nature and structure of these arts, the stories just don't hold up as well. Indeed, some practitioners have given up trying altogether. They have fallen back and retrenched in their defenses. They now inform us that all history is subjective. That no one can really claim to be doing a koryu since times and attitudes have changed. It's rather like the fellow getting caught in a motel with his mistress who, when faced with more and more irrefutable evidence, eventually quits trying to make lame excuses and just whines that "Everybody does it."

Perhaps it is a product of our society of late, when heads of government resort to convoluted explications of the truth and quibble over "what the definition of 'is' is." But there seems to be an awful lot of trying to explain away or rationalize discrepancies of these suspect ryu. There is, too, a tendency on the part of many eager participants to assume a ryu is legitimate and to ignore any evidence to the contrary. "I've made up my mind; don't confuse me with the facts" is a slogan of these types. Instead of explaining the history and principles of their ryu, they now spend much of their time trying to defend them. Real koryu, as I noted in the original article, rarely need this sort of defense. Records are extensive. Lineages are easily available. Only in the West do we have so many koryu that are secret in origin, bereft of any objectively recorded history, and managed by masters who have not a single connection with any known martial art in Japan.

The four premises above all have some veneer of reason. They do not, however, withstand much scrutiny. Begin, if you will, with the suggestions of some that because there is a certain latitude in the exact definition of a koryu, that any and all presuming to be classical arts should be so considered. True, there is some play in the definitions of the ancient and modern martial disciplines of Japan. There is similar play in Western subjects. We can argue reasonably over whether horseshoes or lawn darts are sports, for example. But we cannot, if words have any value at all, engage in a serious argument over whether giving birth is or isn't a sport. It isn't, and tortuous bends and twists of locution, no matter how clever, will not make it so. Just because there is some looseness in the definition

of a koryu should not be taken to mean that there is no definition at all.

There are in Japan at least a couple of organizations devoted to the koryu. The best known is connected with the Bu-
dokan, where it has its own office. If there is no definition of
a koryu, what, we must wonder, do these organizations do?
Why have they certified some ryu and denied admission to
others? Clearly, they have standards and criteria, and while
they may not be foolproof or absolute, an objective classifica-
tion for bujutsu, Japan's classical martial systems, does exist
for them. This seems to bother some in the West. I was in-
formed that conclusions we might reach concerning the status
of a ryu are, at best, "hazarded guesses," and that unless there
is direct contradictory evidence, a determination of truth is
well nigh impossible. Come on. We're getting into the realm
of "You can't prove the Holocaust really happened," here,
aren't we? I can't prove absolutely without a shred of a doubt
that the classical bujutsu are not entirely the creation of a
boatload of Zulu warriors who navigated to Japan and introduced them. (Don't laugh. I've heard explanations that
weren't much less fantastic than this one.) But surely my conclusions on that thesis can be more determinative than a
"hazarded guess." An open mind is one thing. A stubborn refusal to acknowledge a mountain of contrary evidence and a
complete lack of substantiation for a ryu's legitimacy is something else. Sophomoric agnosticism and rhetorical gymnastics
aside, we must on occasion make some judgments. Correct
conclusions are reachable. It's just that they can be tough
when we don't like the direction in which they lead us.

The second argument—that physical skills ought to be a
predominant factor in judging the historical validity of a ryu—
is an appealing one. Initially, it makes some sense. Upon closer

examination, it clearly does not. Those who believe this demonstrate exactly the ignorance of the essential nature of the classical martial ryu that accounts for so many of these misunderstandings in the first place. If we examine the argument, we can see at least three obvious flaws: First, empirical, "direct assessment of someone's skill" is not a reliable indicator of a ryu's authenticity. If you think so, then you'd better be prepared to acknowledge mine as the grand ultimate. I call it "Remington ryu." Haul out your *katana*, your *yari*, your *kusarigama*. Bring 'em all. We'll see how they stack up in close quarters against a 12-gauge pump shotgun. Just because I'd blow the brains out of practitioners of every koryu exponent in Japan is not proof my ryu is an authentic example of a classical combative system of feudal Japan.

Remember; we're talking about schools devoted to arts that lost their practical applicability, in the purest technical sense, centuries ago. Judging their effectiveness is not easy, because we may not always be clear on what it was they were trying to do. Demonstrations of the techniques of any ryu demand a partner trained in them as well. With a willing partner, anyone can look pretty good, pretty effective. This is particularly true when the observer doesn't actually know what to look for. I suppose you could also participate in duels to the death to prove your ryu's efficacy. I'll pass, for obvious reasons, but also because, as with the demonstrations, we'd be getting off the subject. Most martial scholars who question a ryu's lineage are not questioning its methods. They are asking about its provenance. They are interested from a scholarly point of view, not in what the exponents may actually do. The failure to make this distinction speaks volumes of those who would apparently rather not confront it.

Let me give you an example. I pour you a glass of what I suggest is a Côte de Cochon Burgundy, '08. It's one of the great vintages of all time. A bottle costs more than I make in a year. You sip it and ask, reasonably, to take a look at the bottle, to examine the label. "What's the matter," I say. "Doesn't it taste good? Don't you like it?" See how I've changed the subject? You may like it fine, just as a supposed koryu may look very impressive. We're not talking about how it looks or tastes, though. We want some reliable evidence of its history and lineage. This is not unreasonable. And if I were suddenly making up excuses—farfetched excuses at that—for preventing you from looking at the bottle from which I'd just poured, you'd be justified in suspecting I have something to hide about the vintage. Those who brush off any inquiries into the history of their art with pleas of "just come train or watch a practice" are equally suspicious.

Second, as I noted above, the nature of a classical ryu is not always or even often immediately obvious. This is critical. I'm thinking of one koryu I've seen in Japan, which has a silly-looking, exaggerated stepping pattern in many of its kata, the prearranged patterns of action that define the ryu. It looks almost clownish. Not until you learn that these methods were developed for fighting in the muck of rice fields, stepping between rows, does the movement make sense. Koryu often look rather slow, even clumsy, when demonstrated formally. They are in disappointing contrast, in many instances, to what we see on television or in movies. Every time you see a sword fight there, the combatants are jumping around, throwing in kicks, making acrobatic moves that look very effective. Outfit those combatants in the heavy, restrictive armor worn by the samurai at various periods in their history, though, and you'd see that those apparently slow, cumbersome moves of many koryu are perfectly efficient. The kicks and acrobatics would get one killed in a heartbeat. But if you don't know that, you will not make the correct judgment. You must also realize that most koryu contain methods that would be very difficult for you to assess. To those who believe they can examine a koryu and ascertain its practical effectiveness, I would ask, how are you competent to judge such esoterica as blowing a conch shell to signal troop movement? Knotting armor cords so perspiration won't jam them? Handling a serving tray so as to conceal a surprise attack with a hidden dagger? These are methods contained in koryu. Could you look at any of them and tell, with any degree of success, which are correct and which have been made up?

The third and most serious fallacy in this argument was best explained by one reader who insisted that "If it looks like a duck and talks like a duck . . . "

Ducks do not talk where I come from. But I believe his point was that if the practitioners conduct themselves as we think a martial artist should, if they seem to have good skills in the use of some weapons or empty-handed techniques, that is a reliable sign they represent a legitimate koryu. The problem with assigning the title of duck to a beast given the way it walks and talks is that we must have a knowledgeable idea of exactly how it is a duck is supposed to walk and talk.

The classical koryu, I'm sorry to say, are ducks that have been seen by very few people in Japan. Even fewer in the West. If you are reading this, the odds are good you know something about the martial disciplines of Japan, I would even wager you are among the most educated on this subject. Even so, if we were to arrange demonstrations of ten koryu picked at random for an audience of you and other such readers, how many of you could identify even half of the ryu based upon their observation? One percent?

Look at it another way: People, more than once, have mistaken my competency in chado, the art of the tea ceremony. Even people in Japan—those who know nothing about chado—

have made incorrect assumptions about my skills in the art based on observing me at it. I've been taught and have practiced chado basics often enough and long enough to do a reasonable job of the tea ceremony if I must. In the U.S., how many people would spot the flaws in my performance? Almost none. I can look like a competent practitioner of the tea ceremony. But in the presence of a real expert, my mistakes and technical goofs would be recognizable in an instant. We all know of men who've passed themselves off as veterans, who can "talk the talk." They sound as though they were smack in the middle of the Tet Offensive in Vietnam. Put them in a room with real Vietnam veterans and their stories collapse. The real vet knows the right questions to ask.

I know this will be difficult for some readers to swallow because it means acknowledging that we don't know as much as we think we do. I don't mean to be insulting, but most Western enthusiasts of koryu simply do not have enough experience or exposure to these arts to identify the differences between a duck and a goose. The uncritical acceptance of and enthusiastic participation in so many "classical ryu" which are patently fraudulent is distressing proof.

Some readers argued that because they are pleasing themselves and their teachers, and are having a good time, that criticisms of their claims are mean-spirited and irrelevant. It is an argument that fails on at least two counts. First, these questionable koryu are, nearly without exception, demonstrating their art in public places, advertising themselves as inheritors of specific warrior traditions, and presuming to be presenting a part of the martial traditions of old Japan. If they really were off by themselves, engaging in their practice, that might be fine. If you want to go off by yourself and believe that the Confederacy won the Civil War, hey, that's your business. But when you go to a classroom and teach that, or when you present it as fact to impressionable minds, it becomes my concern.

If you were to mount a production of a Noh drama and attempt to pass off the performers as members of a centuries-old school of that drama, members of the Japanese community, the theater world, and any number of Japanese cultural organizations would be rightfully indignant. The same groups would be indignant if you turned out some bowls on a pottery wheel and had a showing of your work, advertising it as being in the tradition of Ogata Kenzan or some other great Japanese potter, when in reality it was nothing even close. Members of the community who have an appreciation for Japanese culture, especially those who have links with a traditional koryu, have a similar right to be angry when those ryu are misrepresented, or when someone dishonestly claims that what they are demonstrating is a classical ryu.

This argument is often accompanied by the assertion that so long as students are having a good time and pleasing their teachers, they won't really mind—and ought not to mind—if their "ryu" was concocted in a basement in Newark a couple of years ago instead of on a battlefield in early Japan. Really? So students who have put in twenty years of effort and money and time, and are told one day that, "Oh, by the way, your teacher just made up all this after watching some samurai movies" shouldn't be upset? After all, if he's had a good time, has practiced sincerely, and uncritically followed his teacher's advice, that should be, runs the argument, the fundamental criteria.

I'm sorry to say that I don't deal with these kinds of students very often. On the contrary, I get letters frequently from students who, when presented with the sad truth of their ryu, are devastated. They have invested enormously, financially and emotionally, in their efforts. To disseminate a fakery is simply cheating. Those cheated are bound to be outraged. If I sell you a "Rolex" you discover to be a fake five years later, I doubt your dissatisfaction would be assuaged by my argument that, well, after all, it has kept perfect time, hasn't it? Imagine a married jerk caught in a motel with his girlfriend. Should he be the husband of someone you know, would you use the same reasoning advocated in this argument with his wife? Gee, Laura, you had a good time in your marriage, you worked on it sincerely, and you were uncritical of your husband's participation in it. Just because he got caught in the sack with his girlfriend shouldn't make you feel bad about the whole enterprise. After all, you didn't do anything wrong.

(One reader, by the way, asserted that if, for instance, you are being told you are learning jujutsu when in fact you are merely being taught modern judo, your time and energies are not wasted because, after all, "good judo is good judo." This is utterly incomprehensible to me, I must admit. It is like contracting to learn Spanish and instead, receiving instruction in German. You ought not complain because, after all, good German is good German.)

Let me be clear. The classical martial koryu of Japan are a profound facet of that nation's heritage. They are a kind of living antique. They are every bit as valuable as works of art in a museum. When fraudulent versions of them are propagated and presented as the real thing, for whatever reason, a kind of cultural vandalism takes place. It is not all that different from defacing a work of art. Or from exhibiting in your own museum objects that aren't what you say they are. You are distorting part of a country's culture. You are claiming, or at least insinuating, that you are a part of a heritage—and presuming to represent it—when you are not. You have no such right. Those who are a part of a koryu should and will take exception to your crime. No one has a right to appropriate the name of an authentic koryu and "teach" methods of any kind, whether they may superficially resemble those of the ryu or not. If they create their own, they should clearly advertise it as such.

Arguments of sophistry, suggesting there can be no objective view of historical subjects like the history of a ryu, are transparent, never advanced by those with facts on their side, always by those who have reached a conclusion and will go to any rhetorical lengths to defend it. Further, while the koryu have a number of good reasons for continuing into the twenty-first century, "making me feel good" is not one of them. The fact that you enjoy your practice of a phony ryu is not a justification for participating in a fraud. Wishing you were a classical bugeisha, conducting yourself as you believe a bugeisha would, are noble motivations. They are not a magical passport, though, that will transform you into a member of a bona fide ryu. If those who have advanced these specious arguments cannot summon up the intellectual integrity to confront their own inconsistencies and irrationalities, a sense of common decency ought to at least give some pause to their advocacy of inauthentic martial ryu.

I'm sure there are those who will disagree, who will continue to take exception to these responses and explanations. They may even be creative enough to come up with some entirely new rationalizations for believing in various deceptions and inaccuracies. I wish them the best of luck.

Heck, as a proud Navy SEAL, I even salute them.

[After this originally appeared in *Furyu, The Budo Magazine of Classical Japanese Martial Arts and Culture*, the editor there, Wayne Muromoto, received a terse letter. It was from an organization that roots out false claimants of fraudulent Navy SEAL Team members. They wished it to be known that there were no official records of a Dave Lowry ever having served on any SEAL Team or having been listed among members of any class of SEAL Team trainees. They requested he publish a retraction of my claim. Seriously. Wayne responded, informing them of what was obvious: The piece was tongue-in-cheek. My claim was preposterous on its face. It was, like, you know, kind of supposed to be "funny." They replied with a letter identical to the first, again demanding a public retraction of my claim. Wayne thoughtfully ignored them. Just to set the record straight: I am not now nor have I ever been a member of a Navy SEAL team. I am, however, participating with a secret, elite squad currently protecting Earth from certain intergalactic forces that seek to enslave our species through brainwashing techniques disguised as music videos . . .]

Kata as a Protection against the Arbitrary

[The following was delivered to the Budo Symposium, in October 2001, at the University of Missouri-St. Louis.]

We were in New Jersey last summer, three of my training partners and I. We were there for a *koshu*, a weekend training clinic, in the Shindo Muso ryu of *jojutsu*. We were imposing on the hospitality of the Skosses, Meik and Diane. Fortunately for all concerned, the renowned Skoss Budo Ranch is a commodious manor; there were about a dozen of us encamped there, along with Mr. Wizard, the remarkably senescent cat in residence, and Phil Relnick. You could tell the latter two apart because Phil moved more than the cat—and having slept in Meik's library next to Phil's room, I can personally attest that Phil snores more loudly than the cat. Relnick sensei is also the first non-Japanese *menkyo kaiden* in the four-plus centuries of the Shindo Muso tradition of the jo. That means he's received the complete transmission of the ryu, been granted all its "secrets," and he's authorized to teach it or even to alter it any way he sees fit. He has been instructing a small group of

Americans here for about the past decade and we were in New Jersey to train with him.

Now, if you know Mr. Relnick, you know he's a talented teacher and a generally affable guy. But he tends, particularly when he's dealing with the frustrations of training the likes of us, a little toward the peripatetic. He gets twitterpated.

If you know Meik, you know he is also extremely gifted as a teacher, certainly among the most skilled martial artists alive today. His proclivities under trying circumstances however, often run toward the—well, what one might say in Japanese—*kuchi ga sugiru*. The best translation is "smart ass."

Given these two personalities, the rather restricted space within the dojo we were using, and the humidity of a New Jersey summer intensified by a thunderstorm approaching one afternoon near the end of the koshu—some kind of conflation was inevitable. Something was going to give.

Relnick sensei had just delivered a rather impassioned soliloquy. Memory fails me as to the exact subject of the offering. I think it had something to do with the utter futility of discerning where he ought to best begin in his criticism of our technique.

Meik raised his hand from a corner of the dojo.

"Sensei."

Phil looked in his direction.

"Sensei," Meik said. "Um, what 'kaddas' do we need to know for our green belt test?"

I am less prepared to answer the fundamental questions regarding the nature of kata than Phil was to answer Meik's smart-ass question. But I'll try to address at least one; one I'm convinced sheds some much-needed light on the subject in general.

Actually, kata has been exhaustively defined (not coincidentally, with the most fervent enthusiasm by those who have the least familiarity with it). It is the "pretty" aspect of budo training. It is a choreographed dance, a pantomime with techniques executed against a phantasmal opponent. It is a convenient implement by which to test students for promotion and to collect fees for same. It was most notoriously dismissed by the sage of the cinematic stir-fried slugfest, Bruce Lee, as "swimming on dry land." When I hear or read these commentaries on kata by such luminaries, I am always reminded of a *Peanuts* comic strip from the mid-sixties. Linus and Lucy, a newspaper spread on the floor between them, are both laughing. "Why are you laughing at that story?" asks Charlie Brown, who's just strolled up. Says Lucy: "Because we don't understand it."

When it comes to the kata, I don't understand it either. If I had to venture my own definition, however, I believe I would steal one from another discipline: Architecture—or, to be more exact, geometry. It was that aspect of mathematics so necessary to his craft that Le Corbusier, the architect, was once asked to define. Geometry is, said Le Corbusier, "a protection against the arbitrary."

Geometry, in a sense, is a recognition of form in a world of nature where chaos is more the norm. It is an awareness of patterns discernible amidst the random. It is a defense, constructed by the human mind, against what would otherwise be erratic and disarticulated. My thought—what I would like to present with merciful brevity here to you today—is that this is also a fundamental definition of kata.

A while back I interviewed Ellis Amdur for *Furyu* magazine—he's the tall guy with less hair than me—who is an authority on de-escalating violent or potentially violent situations in the workplace, in homes, or in schools or hospitals. He talked at length about the mentality needed to behave successfully in stressful situations, whether a mugging or some kind of violent encounter, or a period of battle or warfare. He said that a primary impulse in these conditions is the need to impose some kind of order on them. When I turned on the television on the morning of September 11 and watched the World Trade Center towers destroyed, my initial thoughts were probably very much like yours: It had to be an accident. Or, if not, then some kind of deliberate attack—but from where? What response should we make as a nation? The news that came right after, about another plane hitting the Pentagon, and then another that had crashed in Pennsylvania—it was a morning of near-perfect chaos. And I found myself scrambling to make sense of it all. I was trying to find coherence amidst what was a confusing moment, to say the least. When we human beings are confronted with a chaotic environment of any kind, there is a need—apparently instinctive or nearly so, Ellis had told me—to do just what I was doing. To impose a sense of order upon it. Kata addresses this impulse in an interesting way.

The martial arts practitioner, I need to say, is apt to perceive kata in, I think, far too narrow a perspective. Kata exists in virtually every traditional Japanese art. Some would argue it exists in every sphere of Japanese life as well, a subject for another time and more knowledgeable minds than my own. I have had sufficient exposure to a number of Japanese arts, though, to be confident in noting that none of them is transmitted or inculcated through means other than formal patterns set down meticulously by previous generations. These patterns or shapes are copied assiduously by the following generations until a mastery of the principles behind them is achieved. The student of swordsmanship is engaged in the same process as the practitioner of ikebana or calligraphy. While the techniques may differ, the method does not.

So, to return to the notion that kata is a protection against the arbitrary, how does this protection manifest itself in the various forms of these arts? It does so in different ways. In flower arranging, kata emerges primarily as a spatial response to chaos. The *kadoka* seeks to impose order on nature. The Japanese, incidentally, are given to this kind of imposition, of bracketing nature and contriving to bend it to a definable form. I spend a lot of time in the *Seiwa-en*, the eleven-acre Japanese-style garden we have here at the Missouri Botanical Garden, and I am always amused at comments like, "It looks so natural." That Japanese-style garden—all gardens built according to the kata of Japanese traditional landscape design—is anything but natural. Everywhere you look you see the hand of humans interacting with the plants and other materials in the garden. I was giving a talk there once and casually mentioned the effort expended in pruning some of the pines, pulling away by hand each of the clumps of needles that descend downward, leaving only those that are growing up. One of the women was astounded. "You mean it doesn't grow that way?"

No, pines don't grow that way. Nor do flowers and other natural materials arrange themselves according to the dictates of the many different ryu devoted to ikebana. If you have ever seen ikebana instruction, you will know that the components of the art are initially stacked in big plastic buckets or scattered across a whole room. It looks like someone went nuts while strolling across a landscape, armed simultaneously with a weed-whacker and a chain saw. The flowers and branches and such must be arranged and placed in forms consonant with the principles and teachings of the ryu, all in the brief interval before they wilt and die. It isn't as easy as it looks. It is maddening, in fact, to assemble an arrangement, to make order of chaos, in what you are certain is a form in accordance with the dictates of the lesson, only to have the teacher come around and make corrections that are so apparently minute you can't even see them. It's true that the kadoka's confrontation with chaos is not of a life-threatening nature (unless one counts the occasional impulse to murder the teacher). Even so, it is a struggle, a fight against what is random and disorganized. It is a struggle the kadoka accomplishes primarily by addressing chaos through the mediation of space and dimension. This is one approach to Le Corbusier's concept of "arbitrary"—seeking a protection against it by formulations of arrangement.

There seems little, upon superficial analysis, that is chaotic in chado, the tea ceremony. The tea hut, only four and one half mats in size, is not known for the amount of clutter or knickknacks fustying up the space. Even so, we can again see clear evidence of this encounter with the arbitrary, with the attempt, through an adherence to outer form, to respond to what is capricious and chaotic.

Did your mothers teach you the distinction between being prompt and being on time? If not, it goes like this: Being prompt means arriving at the beginning of an event. Being on time means arriving at the most interesting moment. The tea ceremony is an encounter with timing, arriving at the most interesting moment in each step of the process. One could perform all the *temae*, the "kata" of the tea ceremony, perfectly. Every move in order and in the correct sequence. And still the entire ceremony could be a clumsy exercise. What matters in chado is not just to do a thing right, but to do it with the proper timing. Timing is the principal approach taken by the chado exponent in confronting chaos.

I haven't any experience with Noh theater other than as a spectator. But I did once learn one movement that is common in several of the plays. It consists of coming up from a kneeling crouch and extending an unfolded fan diagonally across one's front. A friend of my teacher's who was an accomplished expert on Noh showed it to me, and I tried for probably half an hour to do it. I never did perform it to his satisfaction. His complaint, again and again as I went through this seemingly simple motion, was that my *choshi*, my rhythm, was off. Actually, what he said was that I was *onchi*, (deaf) to the rhythm. Come on, I'm thinking; it's standing up and swinging a fan out to the side. It was hardly, in terms of kinesiological complexity, a feat of *Swan Lake* proportions. No matter. He wasn't satisfied, and he explained that rhythm is all in Noh. That, I would venture, is the Noh theater's principal response to chaos. Establishing rhythm.

And so it goes. When we begin to examine the particular nature of kata in different Japanese arts, we see again and again an approach to meeting and making order of chaos. Various approaches, to be more exact: spatially, in terms of timing; or dimensionally; or in the sense of the rhythm that concerns the art. All of which brings us back to the budo and its kata. What is the approach the kata of budo take to confronting and making sense of chaos?

I think when we examine kata from this perspective, as a response to chaos, we begin to see at least one reason why the budo are exemplary forms of Japanese art and cultural expression. That's because the kata of the budo seem to encompass or incorporate each of the approaches stressed by the others. They offer dimensions beyond those other arts as well.

Kata of the martial variety offer an opportunity to bring the practitioner into a direct confrontation with chaos. Now sure, the kadoka has a table full of flowers or other plants, and a container, and has to make sense of all those, to impose form that is pleasant, structurally sound, and so on. The tea ceremony is aimed at producing a harmonious kind of timing.

But it would be fatuous to compare this with the physical and mental exercise of martial art kata. I've been soundly scolded for failing to time a tea ceremony movement correctly. I have also taken a *bokuto* to the wrists or a *fukuro shinai* to the side of my head when I didn't do a movement in the dojo correctly. I have never confused the differences in the latter with the errors I have made in the tea ceremony. The kata of a combative art are, by necessity, more intense, more focused. Their consequences, we are frequently reminded if we are training correctly, much more sober.

In addition, though, and more to our point of discussion here, is the fact that martial art kata enlist a wide spectrum of approaches in this matter of confronting chaos. From the very beginning, the student is taught to deal with a range of these approaches. He contends with problems relating to spatial relationships between himself and his opponent. He encounters the timing we spoke of earlier, as well as rhythm. And he does it within a very dynamic arena, one where physical skills figure in, along with mental and emotional talents. I cannot think of another Japanese art in which there are so many paths taken toward the face-off with chaos, nor any arts in which the arbitrary is so dramatically and vividly met.

The kata of a koryu seek to reorganize us on a neurological level. The way we think, Spinoza said, is the way we structure our reality. Kata are designed, brilliantly so, to structure our realities according to principles that enable us to defeat the other guy while keeping ourselves in one piece. The simple-minded interpretation of kata is that it "tells a story." Kata are patterns of combative movement somehow proven efficacious in a combative engagement, goes this interpretation, memorized to equip us to "tell" the story with some measure of success. If that is the real meaning of kata, or even a corollary meaning, then the creators of kata must have been some pretty dumb guys. A reliable construct of events works in literature and movies. If a dozen blackguards surround our protagonist, we may reliably assume the first of these is not going to simply step up and put out his lights—especially not if the protagonist speaks English without using contractions. (I have often wondered if the more than half of my lifetime spent in these arts might better have been devoted to my diction. Have you ever noticed that from Kwai Chang Caine to Mr. Miyagi, those who never use contractions are invincible?) Anyway, real life isn't quite so reliable. The "story" of one fight, one war, one violent encounter, is unique when compared with any other. Establishing kata as a means of reliably relating a story so the wished-for consummation will occur is more than futile. It's disastrous.

I think rather that the kata is at least twofold in its function. It is engineered, as I said, to organize our neurological responses; Hunter Armstrong and some others have written extensively about this. But it also presents us with a framework, a structure for dealing with the chaos of combat. By extension, the lessons of this kind of training translate into the broader spectrum of life.

This is what's so fascinating, from one perspective, about koryu kata. Look, there are only so many ways of hacking someone up with a sword or a *naginata*, or whatever the hell it is the ryu features in its curriculum. And so we read comments on the Internet from people who say, "Well, why don't you illustrate these kata; teach them in open seminars? What's the big deal with keeping all this stuff secret?" These people miss the point of the ryu entirely. More specifically, they miss the point of kata. Kata teach technical skills, true. But that's superficial. At the heart of the kata are methods meant for psychological transformation. The purpose of the ryu is to mold a certain personality. I don't mean in the way Jim Jones or some cults create personalities. I'm speaking not about creating a new personality, but integrating one's own, in very singular, determinate ways. The kata of a ryu are directed at producing a mindset consonant with the principles of the ryu. They inform the disposition of the adherent. You could surely learn them through looking at photos in books or mimicking videotapes. They could be distributed at seminars where all are welcome. It is impossible, however, without the intense personal interaction the exponent has with a teacher, to produce the desired result. Learning the kata as a disparate collection of mechanical responses and initiatives is, as our hero Bruce Lee noted, like learning to swim on dry land. Bruce missed—as do these others who wish, out of some curiosity, to learn kata—the unifying elements of this training that instills a mentality along with physical abilities.

I have some experience in two very different koryu. They differ markedly in terms of their history, in terms of their principles and "worldviews," and their approaches to combat. The study of these two very diverse ryu, or any ryu with such different approaches, is informative, challenging, and full of some dangerous pitfalls. Among the most dangerous of these are that the practitioner will develop some kind of split personality. (More importantly, the corporate personality of the ryu risks damage if its members do not reflect and maintain the unique status of that personality.)

In addition, though, to this neurological and psychological transformation, my suspicion is, as I've said, that kata bring us face-to-face with chaos, with, as Mr. Amdur has said, one of our most fundamental fears. Some examples of how this process works:

One common misconception about the koryu among those who have never entered them is that the emphasis on fundamentals is a stifling period for the beginner, that his enthusiasms are tested by incessant repetitions of basic movements, until he's begging to learn something new. You've all heard stories that emphasize this; the *kodansha* (lyrical storyteller's apprentice) who has to tell the same tale over and over again until he gets bored and leaves his apprenticeship and ends up being required to recite his tale for an audience to get some food. And at that time he learns, when the audience is amazed at his storytelling prowess, that the master was right all along. There's some of this in koryu, to be sure. More likely (at least it's been my experience) that instead of boredom, the principal emotions at the beginning stages of entering a ryu are constant panic and a sense of being overwhelmed with a tsunami of information. Every technique has four or five or six major points you're supposed to remember, and you generally do remember them, right after you've done that part of the technique where they were supposed to be employed. From the day they begin, I think most koryu adepts will tell you, they are quite overwhelmed by all the stuff they're given. They're thrown into a maelstrom of chaos when they walk in the door.

Just about the time the basics have at least been intellectually comprehended, the koryu practitioner gets dumped on again. He's far enough along that the kata, instead of being simple repetitive "dances," begin to acquire some kind of reality. That is, the opponent, always his senior, starts putting a little juice in the proceedings. The cuts are coming in at a fairly whizzing pace. The attacks are sharper, more focused; the junior can feel a sense that if he doesn't respond reasonably correctly, he could very well be injured. He may not literally be fearing for his life—but he's got a few owees and "Son of a . . . !"

to recognize this is serious business. He doesn't have the advantage he once had, of intellectually organizing himself for the movements of the kata. He's in the process of *karada de oboeru*, or "learning with the body." Problem is, his body is still adjusting to the lessons of Algebra I, and he's found himself in a mid-level calculus class. One being taught in Farsi. He knows the sequences of the kata with some competence and can produce them under ideal circumstances. But the circumstances in more advanced training in a koryu are rarely ideal. Training outside, switching kata in the middle to go to another one, training with weapons that require a shift in distancing; all these produce a disorder of one kind or another. It is his task, at this point, to find the patterns within the movement. He is finding order amidst the random. Learning a method of protection against the arbitrary.

This is a lifelong process, I suspect. I know there is the image of the master who can flawlessly perform any kata picked at random from an entire ryu's curriculum. I haven't met him yet. I have met plenty of koryu practitioners I would consider extremely competent and expert, and I've seen every one of them screw up, forget a kata, drop a weapon, you name it. They are in the process we all are in—learning to adapt to what their lives have in store for them, for new experiences, for polishing themselves.

Kata are a means of framing experience, of putting the world into a specific order. "Art," said Saul Bellow, "is order imposed on the chaos of life." This is a function of kata, one in which the kata succeed beautifully, it has been my experience, and I am quite convinced that a training in them, pursued with intensity and correct instruction, is a valuable asset. As valuable for us in the twenty-first century as it was in the fifteenth.

Now, if only I was sure of which ones I need to know to get my green belt.

About the Author

Dave Lowry has been involved in a study of the traditional and modern Japanese martial arts and ways since 1968 and he is among the most prolific of writers on the subject in the West. In addition to eight books on *budô*, he has written for *Karate Illustrated, International Fighting Arts,* and *Inside Karate* and has written a monthly column for *Black Belt* magazine since 1986. He has also written for a number of other magazines including *Playboy, Cosmopolitan,* and *Winds,* the in-flight magazine of Japan Air Lines. His next book is *The Sushi Snob, A Connoisseur's Field Guide to Sushi.*

Lowry lives and writes near St. Louis, Missouri, where he is the restaurant critic for *St. Louis Magazine.*